"In our increasingly pluralist and religiously diverse world where religion is too often a source of division or the justification for violence and extremism, Wogaman offers a much-needed resource. With the wisdom of a seasoned pastor, he models how Christians can constructively engage and learn from people of faith in other religious traditions. This accessible and highly insightful book should not only be required reading for clergy but also be an invaluable book for adult study groups in churches throughout the land."

—Charles Kimball, Baptist minister, Presidential Professor and Director of Religious Studies at the University of Oklahoma, and author of *When Religion Becomes Evil: Five Warning Signs*

"In this book Philip Wogaman brings his vast and significant experience as a Christian pastor into dialogue with the radically interdependent world of the twenty-first century. The result relativizes all religious claims to possess ultimate truth and calls us into a new consciousness in regard to the way we contemplate God. I found this book refreshing, stimulating, challenging, and necessary."

—John Shelby Spong, author of *The Fourth Gospel: Tales of a Jewish Mystic*

"For a millennium we have watched religions in contact as religions in continued conflict leading to long-drawn wars, death, and destruction. The new millennium promises to come to grips with this challenge by exploring how religions could not only coexist but learn from each other and begin an era of peace, mutual understanding, and cooperation. Wogaman's book strengthens this promise, reinforcing faith in pluralism and inclusiveness. This book will inspire people of all faiths and help them to look at their own faith and other faiths in a positive way for creating a better world."

—Sayyid M. Syeed, National Director for the Office for Interfaith & Community Alliances for the Islamic Society of North America

"Professor Wogaman has given us a gift in his well-written and thoughtful approach to interfaith study. This book provides a useful paradigm for teaching comparative religion and is an excellent resource for anyone who is interested in interfaith dialogue as a means to greater self-understanding."

— M. Bruce Lustig, Senior Rabbi, Washington Hebrew Congregation

What Christians Can Learn from Other Religions

What Christians Can Learn from Other Religions

J. PHILIP WOGAMAN

WESTMINSTER
JOHN KNOX PRESS
LOUISVILLE · KENTUCKY

First Edition
Published by Westminster John Knox Press
Louisville, Kentucky

14 15 16 17 18 19 20 21 22 23—10 9 8 7 6 5 4 3 2 1

Book design: Sharon Adams
Cover design by MTW Design

Library of Congress Cataloging-in-Publication Data

Wogaman, J. Philip.
  What Christians can learn from other religions / J. Philip Wogaman.
      pages cm
  ISBN 978-0-664-23837-7 (paperback)
  1. Christianity and other religions. I. Title.
  BR127.W625   2014
  261.2--dc23
                                            2013041196

Most Westminster John Knox Press books are available at special quantity discounts
when purchased in bulk by corporations, organizations, and special-interest groups.
For more information, please e-mail SpecialSales@wjkbooks.com.

To Clark Lobenstine

Contents

4. Learning from Islam   28

The feelings many Christians have about Islam are based on conflicts in the Middle East and acts of terrorism by some fanatical Muslims. That is a pity, because there is much about the world's second-largest religion that is positive and from which we can learn. We can, for example, reexamine how the Christian doctrine of the Trinity relates to monotheism and beliefs about Christ. At the practical level, Islam can lead us to take moral and spiritual disciplines more seriously and to confront economic and nationalistic idolatries more directly.

5. Learning from Hinduism   44

Hinduism can help us be more humble about our views of God, for God the eternal is the center and source of everything in this vast universe, and yet God is present to each of us. From Hinduism we can gain new insight into how people move through stages in their life journey.

6. Learning from Buddhism   63

*Buddhism pushes Christians to see how so much human unhappiness
is based on illusions about what we need to be fulfilled as human
beings. We chase after false goals based on illusory values. Buddha
exemplifies the compassion we can feel for people who are locked
into false desires, leading us to do what we can to contribute to
their enlightenment.*

7. Learning from Chinese Religion   83

*China has gone through vast cultural and political changes in
the post-Mao period. The ancient and formative traditions of
Confucianism and Taoism have reemerged as important influences.
Christians who are grappling with religious and political polarization
may gain insights about civility and wisdom in public life from these
traditions.*

8. Learning from Smaller Groups with Special Memories   93

*The less widespread, but vital, religions of the Jains, Sikhs,
Zoroastrians, and Baha'is offer specific gifts to Christians and
adherents of other faiths. The interreligious conversation is
impoverished when they are neglected.*

9. Learning from Atheism   103

*If religion represents our deepest beliefs, then even atheism can be
considered a religion. Christians can learn from early Marxism the
lesson of not allowing faith to be the "opiate" that distracts us from
reality. Twenty-first-century atheists push us to reexamine the dark
side of our faith traditions and to be open to scientific findings about
the universe and our place in it.*

10. Can Other Religions Learn from Christianity?   118

*If Christians can learn from other religions, the reverse is also true.
This chapter does not conclude that people of other faiths must
abandon their existing commitments, but it offers suggestions
about major Christian emphases that can enrich those commitments.*

Preface

*P*eople in various religious traditions have often been insulated from those perceived to be different. But in a world of instantaneous communication and rapid travel, contacts and competitions among religions are no longer avoidable. Historically, such contacts have often led to bloody conflicts and brutal repression, including genocide. The growing interreligious contacts in the twentieth and twenty-first centuries have not lessened the brutalities; in some respects they have increased. That is despite the goodwill proclaimed and practiced by many people, perhaps a large majority of people, in all religions.

Some of the causes of the friction are political and economic; some are the legacy of old grievances and inherited cultural patterns not based on the religions themselves. But there remain unresolved conflicts of basic beliefs and values. That is particularly the case when adherents consider their own faith to be absolutely true and other religions altogether false and misleading. By contrast, universal faiths are generally taken to apply to all people everywhere, regardless of their own beliefs and values.

Even people who are not religious fanatics may find it difficult to see anything particularly attractive in faiths other than their own. As the nineteenth-century English writer George Grote wrote in *The History of Greece*, "It is of course impossible for anyone to sympathize fully with the feelings of a religion not his own." And yet there is bound to be some truth and goodness in all the faith traditions that have claimed people's allegiance over long periods of time. There are religious traditions that have nurtured hundreds of millions or even billions of people over thousands of years. How are we to understand that basic point? Can better understanding of other faith traditions lead to better understanding of our own? Can positive appreciation of other faiths contribute to peace, both in local communities and in the wider world?

I believe so. It seems to me that one helpful exercise is to search for aspects of other faith traditions that expand or clarify or reinforce meanings in one's own.

Undertaking that task, I have sought in this book to ask what I, as a Christian, can learn from several of the other world religions. In some cases, this may be to expand the meaning of Christian faith as held and practiced in the early twenty-first century. At other points, it may be to clarify misunderstandings of Christian faith by people of other religious views and even by Christians themselves. Occasionally it can help us to ferret out the points where time-bound cultural biases and misconceptions have clouded the true nature of our faith.

It is beyond the scope of this small book to deal with all the world's religions or to provide a complete exposition of any of them. In the main, I've stuck to the largest and oldest ones, but the reader should remember that there are other religions embraced by appreciable numbers of people. Perhaps this book will lead others to explore the values of faith traditions that I did not examine here.

Readers may be surprised to discover that I have included atheism as a religion to be mined for its contributions to Christian believers. That may annoy any atheists who happen upon this book! One atheist consultant, after reading an early draft of my chapter on atheism, made that point emphatically. But, as I have defined religion in the first chapter, atheism often qualifies. Apart from occasional opinion surveys, we cannot know how many atheists there are, nor, for that matter, how many different versions of atheism exist. We do know that atheism has become a significant force in the modern world, especially in North America and Europe. So it is included here.

Readers should note that this book does not attempt to provide a full account of the religions I have considered. A full understanding of each of these religions would require many more pages. But that is not the point of this book. What I have sought to offer here is a better sense of what we can learn from other faiths, which is a much more selective look at the different religious traditions. This is a venture of interpretation: not only interpreting selected aspects of the religions from which we can learn but also interpreting important aspects of the Christian faith itself. Not everybody will agree with the interpretations offered here, but I hope this venture will lead to deeper thought and conversation about what we can all learn from one another.

While the book is intended primarily for Christians, I am encouraged by contacts with adherents of other faiths to hope that others may find this helpful as well. No doubt my Hindu or Muslim friends will feel that their traditions have been presented too incompletely and that, indeed, one almost has to be a Hindu or a Muslim to treat those religions adequately. I am reminded of a conversation with a Buddhist friend more than a decade ago when I shared my sermon "What Christians Can Learn from Buddhism." His response: "That was all right—for a Christian." While I've learned a good deal more about Buddhism since that day, he might say the same thing now. Still, the adherents of the religions explored here may find this an intriguing invitation to deepen their own understandings. I would be delighted to see non-Christians write books like this about what their traditions can learn from others.

I offer some preliminary observations in the first chapter. The chapters that follow successively examine what Christians can learn from primal religion, Judaism, Islam, Hinduism, Buddhism, Chinese religions, and atheism. Chapter 8 will deal with the somewhat less prominent religions of Jainism, Sikhism, Baha'i, and Zoroastrianism.

In writing this book, I wish to thank the congregation of Foundry United Methodist Church in Washington, DC, for patiently enduring a preliminary version of this volume in a series of sermons more than a decade ago. Later I taught a course on Christian ethics and world religions at the Wesley Theological Seminary in Washington, and I found the diverse groups of students and visiting lecturers from different faiths helpful. As a member of the founding board of the Interfaith Alliance and the board of InterFaith Conference of Metropolitan Washington, DC, I learned much from colleagues of different religions, including some religious traditions I had known scarcely anything about. More recently, I am indebted to the people of the Claremont School of Theology in Claremont, California, for the stimulation and contacts afforded by the school's exciting new Claremont Lincoln University project in cooperation with Jewish and Muslim institutions (anticipating participation by still other faith groups).

I have, additionally, made presentations to and received helpful suggestions from individuals and groups, including the Colesville Presbyterian Church of Silver Spring, Maryland; the Dumbarton and Metropolitan Memorial United Methodist Churches of Washington, DC; the Westminster Presbyterian Church of Alexandria, Virginia; the retired clergy group of the Baltimore-Washington Conference of the United Methodist Church; the Osher Lifelong Learning Institute of American University; social studies and world religions teachers of the Fairfax County, Virginia, high schools; the InterFaith Conference of Metropolitan Washington; the Interreligious Council of American University; and a study group in the Adirondack village of Long Lake, New York. The people who have participated in these conversations are too numerous to list here, but I want to express particular thanks to several people, representing my own and other faith traditions, who have read all or part of this book, thereby significantly improving the end product. None of these readers are to be held responsible for remaining problems and misunderstandings, but they can be thanked for helping me to make this a better book. So, my special thanks to Sayyid Syeed, Dan Sackett, Pamela Theimann, Roger Gilkeson, Aaron Kiely, D. C. Rao, Bill Aiken, Neal Christie, Jihad Turk, Sathianathan Clarke, Clark Lobenstine, Charles A. Kimball, Barbara Brown Zikmund, and my Westminster John Knox Press editor, Dan Braden.

These experiences and contacts have taught me that while we must learn much from one another at an intellectual level, in the end our personal contacts and friendships may prove even more important. Still, the intellectual level remains important. Understanding what other faiths can teach us can help us forge friendships with persons whose religions are different from ours, and I believe that greater understanding of other faiths contributes to better understanding of our own.

A special word of thanks, once again, to my wife, Carolyn, who, for more than half a century, has taught me important lessons about openness and compassion.

I have dedicated this book to the Rev. Clark Lobenstine, with appreciation for his friendship and for his more than thirty years as Executive Director of the InterFaith Conference of Metropolitan Washington. Through these years of creative leadership, he has inspired people of very different religious traditions to learn from one another.

Chapter 1

Learning from Other Religions

Pitfalls and Possibilities

> *Jesus said to him, "I am the way, and the truth, and the life. No one comes to the Father except through me. If you know me, you will know my Father also."*
>
> —*John 14:6*

> *Jesus said to him, "Why do you call me good? No one is good but God alone."*
>
> —*Mark 10:18*

*B*efore addressing what Christians can learn from other religions, we must ask whether that is even a legitimate topic. Any number of Christians doubt that there is anything to be learned from people who have not accepted Christ and become a part of his church. A favorite scriptural quotation comes readily to mind: "I am the way, and the truth, and the life. No one comes to the Father except through me" (John 14:6). If Jesus is *the* way, what could there be in other religions for people who follow the way of Jesus? Don't people of other religions have to be brought to this light? Isn't the really important question the reverse of the title of this book, that is, what can people of other religions learn from Christians? And isn't the basic answer to that question the fundamental one: how they can learn about and come to accept Christ? But not so fast!

There are two reasons why Christians cannot take that passage from the Fourth Gospel as a sufficient basis for rejecting everything about other faiths. The first is that there is more than a little doubt whether Jesus himself ever uttered those words. The Gospel of John was the last of the four Gospels in the New Testament to be written. Most New Testament scholars date the writing to sometime during the 90s CE, at least sixty years after Jesus' crucifixion. The earlier Gospels and the writings of Paul convey a very high

1

conception of Christ, but they do not offer a view of Christ as the only way to God. Most New Testament scholars doubt whether the apostle John, or anyone else who actually knew Jesus, wrote the Gospel of John. That is not to say that the Fourth Gospel is without merit, but it must be taken for what it is: a theological interpretation of the meaning of Christ. In some respects, the writing is brilliant, but, in common with most theological writings, it must be studied with care.

The other reason for not considering this a basis for rejecting everything about other faiths is that even those who take the words at face value must then ask themselves, what is it *about* Christ that makes him the most important way to God? For instance, one could interpret the passage to mean that it is the love of Jesus that shows the way. The John 14 passage continues, "If you know me, you will know my Father also. From now on you do know him and have seen him." To experience Jesus, especially the love of Jesus, is to see what God is like. If God is God of love, then the way to God is through love, the kind of love displayed by Jesus himself. That leads to further questions: Is it possible that something of that love can be discovered in adherents of other religions? And is it possible that one can discover in those other settings insights that might illuminate even the way of Jesus?

John Wesley's concept of prevenient grace could help here. Wesley considered grace to be, in many respects, the most basic of all Christian doctrines. Grace is the boundless love of God, illustrated most fully in the person of Christ. Those who have encountered and accepted this grace in Christ have experienced what Wesley called justifying grace. Even those who have experienced justification by faith in this grace must continue on a journey of being perfected in love. Wesley called this sanctifying grace. Prior to justification and sanctification, there is prevenient grace, meaning the grace that comes *before* encountering and accepting Christ. Prevenient grace is a recognition that the God of love is already at work everywhere, not just among Christians.

Christians can ask whether they might learn more about this prevenient grace as it is manifested in other religions—and, taking that a step further, whether a deeper understanding of other religions can contribute to a richer, truer perspective on Christ himself.

Pitfalls in Comparing Religions

Is it even possible to compare religions? In a sense, it obviously is possible—and in this book it is necessary. But there is one immediate problem. How can the adherents of one faith know enough about other religions to arrive at accurate comparisons? Isn't religious knowledge possible only from the inside? That may be so, at least up to a point. People of one religion seeking to characterize another cannot know what it is like to *experience* the other faith. Will the criteria of judgment be drawn from one's own faith experience? Does that distort the lens?

If religions are offered as universal, then some understanding of faiths other than one's own cannot be entirely excluded. One should be able to locate points of agreement and disagreement that are not entirely off the mark. As in this book, it should be possible to explore the points at which one can learn from other traditions, even while retaining commitment to one's own.

There is another hazard to be avoided. Sometimes, when criticizing other religions, we compare the *best* in our own faith with the *worst* in others. If we compare "our" ideals with "their" practices, we will have unfairly judged the other faith tradition. In his insightful portrait of Muhammad, Omid Safi states this point emphatically: "One of the most common mistakes made in cross-religious conversations is that people end up comparing the loftiest and noblest aspects of their own tradition with the most hideous aspects of others." He asks how Christians would feel if their faith tradition were defined by the closing words of Psalm 137, "Happy shall they be who take your little ones and dash them against the rock," or the reference in Numbers 15:36 to a man who was stoned to death for gathering sticks on the Sabbath, or the lines in Ephesians 5 and elsewhere requiring women to be subservient to men. Most Christians would say that such passages are taken out of context or that they do not represent what the faith is really about. But couldn't representatives of other faiths make the same point about similarly objectionable quotations from their scriptures?

Every one of the world's religions has enough truth and goodness in it to have been attractive to large numbers of followers. Every one of them has also had a dark side, fueled by fanaticism and, sometimes, by self-interest. We must not compare the bright side of our faith with the dark side of others.

Or the other way around. In the emerging interreligious dialogues of our time, some participants have thought that to sustain the dialogue they must be entirely negative about their own faith traditions to demonstrate their tolerance in conversation with others. But openness toward others does not require rejection of one's own tradition. Real dialogue is from strength of conviction, combined with respect for and openness toward the convictions of others.

Then there is the pitfall of out-and-out syncretism, the notion that it is possible to blend all religions and emerge with something better than any of them taken singly. Such efforts are often so bland that the end product is somewhat *less* than what the various religions, taken on their own terms, have to offer. A case in point is the Golden Rule—do unto others as you would have them do unto you. That idea, with some variations, can be found in most of the great world religions, and that point of convergence is to be celebrated. Still, there is more to the various religions than that, including the differing theological contexts. We can welcome common values and beliefs while remaining skeptical that complete synthesis of different religions will ever be possible. Certainly the present volume does not anticipate such an outcome. Perhaps even more to the point, the differences *within* each of the major religions frustrate efforts at synthesis beyond one's own faith.

Further, as we seek to learn from other religions, we must remember that some beliefs and practices that we associate with another tradition are often an expression of social customs and political forces having little or nothing to do with the religion itself. Attitudes toward women in a number of Muslim countries and the caste system in India may illustrate this problem, as would the medieval Inquisition in predominantly Christian lands. It can be difficult to assess the interplay between religious views and political and cultural commitments.

Such issues were discussed vigorously in the early to mid-twentieth century. A robust Christian missionary movement had developed during the nineteenth century, with thousands of missionaries going from Europe and North America to countries such as China and Japan and the largely colonial territories of Asia and Africa. The intent was to convert the millions of Asians and Africans from other religious backgrounds. The Student Volunteer Movement, inspired by John R. Mott, motivated large numbers of college students to set aside other career objectives and enlist as missionaries determined to evangelize the world in one generation. An ecumenical missionary movement gave rise to world missionary conferences in 1928 (Jerusalem) and 1938 (Tambaram, India) at which there were serious reappraisals of Christian missions and their relationship to other world religions.

The discussions and writings of this period prior to the Second World War anticipate, to a striking degree, today's debates. The major difference between that time and today is the transformation of former colonial territories of Africa and Asia, with more than a billion people changing their status from colonial subjects to citizens of new nations. Major non-Christian religions that had been on the defensive gained new self-confidence. Christian missions continued, but now there were also representatives of Hinduism and Buddhism establishing a presence in North America and Europe and spreading their influence in so-called first-world settings.

Changing Perspectives on the Christian Mission

The earlier twentieth-century discussions about the relationship between Christianity and other world religions remain strikingly relevant as representatives of different religions face one another on a more equal footing, although not many Christians today are familiar with those discussions.

The Laymen's Foreign Missions Inquiry of the late 1920s and early 1930s, headed by Harvard philosopher William Ernest Hocking, attempted a sweeping review of the Christian missionary enterprise to non-Christian parts of the world. Its conclusions, published in 1932, were not hostile to missions, but they did break new ground in their positive attitude toward other religions. The report by the inquiry's Commission of Appraisal concluded that all the world's religions have values that should not be rejected, even though Christianity remains unique. God is present everywhere, so we must not disregard that presence in religions other than our own. The report called for a renewal of Christian life as a living faith and a relative de-emphasis of abstract doctrine and exclusive conceptions of the institutional church.

The inquiry stated the attitude of Christians toward other faiths in a new way: "The mission of today should make a positive effort, first of all to know and understand the religions around it, then to recognize and associate itself with whatever kindred elements there are. . . . It is clearly not the duty of the Christian missionary to attack the non-Christian systems of religion—it is his primary duty to present in positive form his conception of the way of life and let it speak for itself." Far from denying what is essential to Christianity, however, the Laymen's Inquiry sought "with people of other lands a true knowledge and love of God, expressing in life and word what we have learned through Jesus Christ, and endeavoring to give effect to his spirit in the life of the world."

The conclusions of the Laymen's Inquiry were not accepted by everybody, of course, and they would remain controversial today. The Dutch theologian Hendrik Kraemer illustrates the negative reaction during the mid-twentieth century with his sharp contrast between Christian faith and all other religions. According to Kraemer, the various religions represent human striving. They are a human achievement, often very impressive, even noble. But, like ventures in philosophical thinking, they ultimately fall short because they do not provide an answer to the deepest human problem. The fundamental problem is that we are sinners; in our darkness, in our despair, we cannot create our own way out of the pit. In Kraemer's view, Christian faith alone promises real hope in our hopelessness. It is faith not in our ability to think or create or act, but in the revelation that God has initiated our salvation through Christ. God's action, not ours, is our only hope.

These contrasting points of view about non-Christian religions are still present in twenty-first-century Christianity. The main purpose of this book is to test whether other religions have anything to offer Christians. Clearly, the way we view this question has important implications for Christian missionary activity. Should the primary effort of missions be to proselytize, or are there other purposes?

I was briefly involved in the Methodist missionary movement in the early 1960s. That was a time of rapid, even revolutionary, change in parts of the world where most of the missionary activity was located. In 1960, my wife and I had accepted the invitation to serve as missionaries in Cuba, where I was to be a seminary professor. Because of the Cuban Revolution led by Fidel Castro, we weren't able to take up that post. Instead, we returned to New York, where I assisted in the development of a program of long-range planning for our Board of Missions. Thus, I had a front-row seat on the possibilities and dilemmas of missionary thinking during an unusually turbulent era.

In a few short years, a billion people had changed their political status from colonial domination to independence. Sometimes independence movements emphasized indigenous non-Christian religions. Often missionaries were rejected as tools of colonial domination. Some missionaries were able to adjust creatively; others were not. When one of our executives returned from an extended visit to missions in Africa, he asserted that half of the missionaries there were doing more harm than good; fortunately, he believed, the other half more than made up for the others. The church, however, was already planted almost everywhere. So the missionary task was less one of making new converts and more one of providing assistance to existing churches. In non-Christian settings that could mean participating in interreligious forms of cooperation. I do not recall that any of us felt particularly threatened by that.

This situation of a half century ago has been reinforced by developments in subsequent years, particularly as the mainline denominations and ecumenical movements have continued to reassess the missionary task and the possibilities of interfaith dialogue and cooperation. No longer do these churches and ecumenical bodies think of the central missionary task as gaining converts from other faiths. That is not exactly the view of more evangelical and Pentecostal churches. Indeed, one of the most striking evidences of this is the growth of such churches at the expense of Roman Catholicism in Latin America.

Another new phenomenon is the increasing number of missionaries from other countries at work in North America and Europe, establishing something of a two-way street. Representatives of non-Christian religions, especially from Asia, are gaining converts and establishing communities of faith in North America and Europe.

What Is Religion?

Basic to the current differences of opinion among Christians is the very definition of religion itself. Should we, following Hendrik Kraemer, sharply contrast religion with Christian faith? The problem here, as any student of world religions will recognize, is that claims of revelation are not unique to Christians, although the forms of revelation claims vary from one religion to another. For example, Muslims emphasize God's direct revelation to humanity through the transmission of the Qur'an (literally word by word) to Muhammad, and Buddhists speak of the Buddha's moment of enlightenment.

If unique revelation claims are the basis of comparison among religions, how are we to know which claims are true and which are misleading? Christians can appeal to God's ultimate disclosure in God's own time or to the Romans passage that says, "When we cry, 'Abba! Father!' it is that very Spirit bearing witness with our spirit that we are children of God" (Rom. 8:15b–16). We are left then with spiritual discernment, which may indeed be the decisive evidence in support of any faith. But the role of the mind in sorting out the differences among revelation claims cannot so easily be dismissed. Any number of conflicting religious traditions—some of which cannot stand the test of time or moral adequacy—have been deeply satisfying to their adherents' spiritually.

Paul Tillich defined religion as our "ultimate concern," and that is not a bad way to frame a definition. Religion is what concerns us ultimately; it is what we care about most deeply; it is what matters most to us. In a similar vein, partly derived from Hebrew tradition, we can define our religion in terms of what we value most, which is to say, what we worship. By such definitions, it is evident that to be human is to have some form of religion. So religion cannot be defined by any particular conception of God or of gods, and, as we have suggested above, even atheism can be described as a religion. Indeed, a person's *professed* religion may not even be his or her *real* religion! A person could profess belief in God (as expressed in the Bible or other sacred scripture) while actually being more devoted to nationalism or even crass materialism. In *The Prince*, Machiavelli offered the cynical advice that a ruler must, above everything else, *appear* to be religious. But it is clear that the real religion of the aspiring ruler would be gaining and holding power. Are there people of our time whose passion in life is the gaining and holding of great wealth? Or status? Or power?

Another important twentieth-century theologian, H. Richard Niebuhr, explores how all of us have a "center of value" that defines all our lesser values. The highest value, to him, is "radical monotheism," in which our center of value is also the source of all being. But he notes that many people are activated by what he calls henotheism, which is worship of one's own group. That could be one's family, one's nation, one's racial or ethnic group, and so on. It could even be one's church, if that is a group to which one is devoted while excluding all others.

The point here is that what we profess as our religion may not be what we value most. Some of the most murderous interreligious conflicts of our time illustrate this henotheism a good deal more than the faith that is held formally by the people involved.

It follows that not everything we call religion really *is* religion. If what we value most is not the same thing as what we profess, then the profession is not religious. It is only appearance. And, of course, many of our values, while sincerely held, are not religious either, for we do not center our lives on them. I may value a beautiful painting or musical composition without worshiping it. A friendship can be very important to us, but not the center of our lives. Almost anything imaginable could become all-important to us, but most things do not rise to that level. Chapter 9 on atheism will raise the question of definition in a somewhat different way.

Which leaves us where we started in approaching all religions, including our own, both respectfully and critically. Religion, thus understood, truly is a spiritual concern. But that does not mean that it cannot be discussed in intellectual as well as spiritual terms. The point expressed in the title of this book remains both legitimate and urgent.

Confronting the Great Unknown

If religion is conceived, following Tillich, as our ultimate concern, we will never have enough external evidence to validate its claims. An atheist friend challenged me with a serious question: "If there is a God, why couldn't he just once make that unmistakably clear by writing a message in the sky, or something like that?" I responded that if that were to happen, my friend, as the scientist that he was, would immediately think of explanations for such a strange phenomenon—perhaps a skywriting airplane or an unusual configuration of clouds.

My friend also had to confront the limits of his own knowledge. The problem is underscored by a scientific view of the unknown. It is not simply that what is unknown will in due course become known through the relentless progress of science. Indeed, science will doubtless continue to explore uncharted areas that are currently beyond its understanding, and many explorations will doubtless be successful. The problem is that the more we come to know, the more we know that we don't know! In a provocative book, astrophysicist Edward Harrison concludes that

> as knowledge grows, new facts and fresh ideas cast shadows of uncertainty over old facts and ideas. Previous knowledge must repeatedly be revised and reinterpreted. In time the new knowledge inevitably reaps the harvest of further doubt. Uncertainty becomes one's constant companion. Learned ignorance—awareness of ignorance—like entropy seems never to decrease but always increase. It urges us to seek certainty by acquiring greater knowledge, which when attained, unfailingly creates further uncertainty. Solve one problem and you create many more. . . .
>
> The more we enlarge knowledge the more aware we become of our ignorance. . . .
>
> Beyond all systems stands the Universe in a cloud of unknowing.

The astrophysicist who wrote those words was thinking primarily about our knowledge of phenomena—that is, what we can know about the nature and source of things. What is matter, ultimately? What is energy? What about the origins of life? What about the big bang? It is the proper business of science to keep probing these questions. But we also confront the unknown in more directly human terms. What is the meaning of our lives? Is our experience of moral freedom only an illusion? How are we to understand our relationships? Most of all, what are we to think of the truly ultimate question: does the universe reflect a divine purpose? While Harrison does not probe those issues, here, too, we confront the cloud of unknowing, if by knowledge we mean what we know for sure.

Does this leave us in a cloud of pessimism? I don't think so. I would prefer to frame it like this: Think of everything we know as being contained within a circle. Beyond the circle is the great unknown. As we add to our knowledge, the circle expands. That does not deny the knowledge we have within the expanding circle. But it means that the outer circumference of the circle has greater contact with the unknown.

What Is Revelation?

More than that, we are led to conclude, with the New Testament book of Hebrews, that our religious relationship with this vast unknown must indeed depend on faith of some kind; as its author asserts, "Faith is the assurance of things hoped for, the conviction of things not seen. . . . By faith we understand that the worlds were prepared by the word of God, so that what is seen was made from things that are not visible" (Heb. 11:1, 3). We grasp the unknown through some form of revelation. That does not have to mean a thundering voice from beyond or the flawless words of a sacred writing. It certainly does not have to set aside the factual knowledge we already have, including the dependable conclusions of rigorous science and what commonsense experience may tell us. We will consider some aspect or aspects of actual experience to disclose this "ultimate" that lies beyond all experience.

Revelation is, in that sense, metaphorical. It always points beyond itself. Even natural theology (such as that expressed by ancient Stoics and later philosophies) cannot claim to have certain knowledge. We never have access to the whole of reality. Put in a different way, we are all dependent on those aspects of experience that bring all life into focus. Claims that are inconsistent with observed experience or self-contradictory are open to criticism. While I was writing this book, an elderly participant in a discussion group I was conducting came up with a direct way to characterize this view of revelation. It is an "aha" moment, she said. It's what helps make sense of everything else.

This understanding of the meaning and necessity of revelation underscores the importance of interreligious dialogue as we probe understandings of revealed truth that are different from our own. The task is not only legitimate; it is necessary. What "makes sense" can be different to different people, even within the same religion, and much more so among people of different religious backgrounds. I am convinced that those of us who are Christian can indeed learn from other religions, even though our openness does not require us to accept beliefs and practices that are contrary to our own experience or to the best in our own tradition. Our attitude toward other faiths cannot be either wholesale agreement or total rejection.

We turn, then, to the task of identifying particular points of non-Christian religions from which we can learn. This task is not only legitimate and necessary; in our time it has become urgent.

Questions for Discussion

1. Does openness to learning from other religions strengthen or weaken Christian faith?

2. Should Christian churches send missionaries to non-Christian lands? Should missionaries from non-Christian religions be welcomed in predominantly Christian countries?
3. Do you agree or disagree with the author's definitions of religion and revelation?
4. If what we value most is central to who we are, what are we to make of the relationship between materialism and religious faith in American culture?
5. Can you think of persons or groups whose actual religion is not the same as what they profess?
6. Can you think of illustrations of persons or groups who compare the best of their own faith tradition with the worst of others?

Chapter 2

Learning Afresh from Primal Roots

They had what the world has lost: the ancient, lost reverence and passion for human personality joined with the ancient, lost reverence and passion for the earth and its web of life. Since before the Stone Age they have tended that passion as a central, sacred fire. It should be our long hope to renew it in us all.

—John Collier

*T*his comment voices deep appreciation for the religious perspective of the people whom John Collier had come to know through his work as U.S. commissioner of Indian affairs. The often-sorry record of Anglo Americans in dealing with the original inhabitants of North America has blinded many Christians to what they could learn from those whose spiritual roots long preceded the time of Christ. The original inhabitants of Africa, Australia, and the Americas have strikingly similar religious views. As Christians seek to learn from other religions, they do well to attend first to the very earliest expressions of human spirituality.

Humanity's Earliest Religious Expressions

We begin with the very oldest religious traditions. I will follow Huston Smith in referring to these as primal, because they came first. Some have described these religions as primitive, indigenous, tribal, or aboriginal. I generally avoid those terms because they are either pejorative or confusing. These are the religions associated with preliterate cultures of the Americas, Australia, Africa, and various islands. Their origins are prehistoric, perhaps by tens of thousands of years, and yet they continue to exist here and there around the world. They have, for centuries, been the object of intense

12

missionary work by the major religions. Often efforts to convert the followers of primal religions have been successful. But elements of the primal religions have subtly continued in the beliefs and practices of those who have been converted.

Is that, at least in some respects, a good thing? Can Christians also learn from primal religions? Do such religions even have enough in common to answer the question? Such religions are isolated from one another. The Aborigines of Australia had no contact, at least none that we are aware of, with native tribes of North America. South American tribes were remote from the cultures of Africa. Southeast Asian cultures had no contact, so far as we know, with cultures in far-off Siberia or Canada and probably not much with the Pacific islands. And so on. Are there enough themes common to the widely separated primal cultures to invite discussion of what we can learn from them? The short answer is yes.

Unlike the religions often classified as "major," the primal religions have not been transmitted by sacred written texts. No scriptures, no Bible, no Qur'an, no written theologies or commentaries. Instead, traditions have been maintained through the generations orally and by ritualistic practices and rites of initiation. Accustomed as we are to flawed memories and garbled accounts of events, we may not give enough credit to the extraordinary feats of memory of peoples who have not preserved their histories in written form. Our literature, and now the Internet, has allowed us to rely on such sources outside ourselves. We ask, why should I memorize that poem or that narrative or that sacred teaching when I can always look it up on the Internet or in the library? Perhaps we've become lazier. Or at least, we may have forgotten the importance of what is stored in our brains.

Sometimes we learn the value of memory in unexpected settings. In a book about his experience as a prisoner of war in Germany during World War II, theologian Roger Shinn tells how he was able to stay alert during weeks when he was held in isolation. On the walls of his room he wrote scriptural verses and hymns and poems as he remembered them. He had no access to books—and there was no Internet to consult! He was unable to converse with others; there were no classes, no seminars. It came down to what he had stored up in his brain, and that result was quite impressive even to him. He had grown up during a time when memorizing things was emphasized; many of those childhood memories had never been lost. That was also true of my own childhood. We memorized psalms and other Scriptures in vacation Bible school; we learned to sing hymns from memory. In later life, I can recite the lines of many hymns as a result of having sung them so often through the years.

The storehouse of memory is an immeasurably important resource as we confront new problems and as we interact with one another in a shared religious tradition. This does not mean that we should abandon literature and the wonderfully accessible Internet. Nevertheless, we can learn something from the primal religions about the values and dependability of oral transmission and about how myths and stories can convey truth.

Pervasive Spiritual Presence

What about the focal point of worship? Is primal religion polytheistic? In a perceptive response to that question, Huston Smith comments that primal religion is not at all like the polytheisms of ancient Europe, with their Jupiters and Athenas and Marses. It is implicitly monotheistic. Smith quotes a Navajo, Carl Gorman, who asserts that in Navajo traditional culture "the Supreme Being is not named because he is unknowable. He is simply the Unknown Power." Primal religions commonly view all aspects of reality in spiritual terms. So there are the spirits of trees and rivers and mountains— and of all the plants and animals. Rituals of communing with these spirits can appear to be polytheistic, and that may sometimes be the case. And sometimes such polytheism can express superstition—as in a fear of malevolent spirits lurking behind things or even of the ability of some people to destroy their enemies by invoking evil spirits through curses.

There may be a deeper sense in which the spiritualizing of all things is an expression of the spiritual interconnectedness of all reality. Smith quotes an interpreter of Native American tribal religion:

> No object is what it appears to be, but it is simply the pale shadow of a Reality. It is for this reason that every created object is *wakan*, holy, and has a power according to the loftiness of the spiritual reality that it reflects. The Indian humbles himself before the whole of creation because all visible things were created before him and, being older than he, deserve respect.

Everything is spiritually interconnected. An African theologian puts it this way: "Africans in general recognize and operate on this truism: the universe is an organic system. . . . All beings (entities) are inextricably interrelated, and thus impact each other."

Such insights are not alien to the Christian faith, but they can be discarded easily when we treat some objects as being outside the province of God. From a spiritual standpoint, much of reality is enfolded in mystery. Yet, if God is Creator and Sustainer of all being, then *nothing* is alien to

God. From a moral standpoint, the interconnectedness of all beings means that our actions have consequences far beyond their immediate setting. Our actions, like pebbles tossed into a pond, create ripples that affect the whole surface, to the farthest shore. This interconnectedness means that all people everywhere are our sisters and brothers, and that relationship, according to much primal religion, extends to other living beings, even the animals we see fit to kill and eat. Our interconnectedness with all things extends over time as well. There is, in primal religion, a deep sense of connection with ancestors. This often includes a special respect for the elders of the tribe as an invaluable source of wisdom.

We must not romanticize primal religion at such points, because murderous conflict—including even cannibalism—among tribes has not been unknown, and superstitious fears can be very real in such settings. The spiritual interconnectedness of everything has important lessons for us, but this does not require us to repudiate scientific insights into material forms of interconnectedness.

A deep insight of primal religion is the interconnectedness of the spiritual and the material. Reverence for the earth, with its teeming forms of life and natural wonders, is not seen as materialism. In learning from this, Christians do not have to follow much primal religion in endowing inanimate forms of nature with specific spirits, and the earth is not itself the ultimate form of reality. It is not God. But all aspects of nature can be seen as having spiritual significance, for they are alike gifts of the creative providence of God.

Such a view has consequences. We can no longer view the earth simply as an instrument for human purposes. It is not simply to be exploited. True, we must use earth's resources—there is no escaping that, if we are to be fed, clothed, sheltered, and transported. We do not have to repudiate technological inventiveness, at least not all of it. But even as we make use of the earth's abundance, we can learn from the primal religions to do so with reverence. For instance, we can learn from Native American hunters who would thank the deer and bison for giving up their lives to feed the human hunters and their families. Later in this book we will encounter some religious views that are opposed to eating flesh from animals. Most Christians do not go that far. Even so, primal respect for all of life can inform the way poultry and livestock are raised and treated.

Moreover, respect for the earth has vast implications for how we work to conserve the future of the planet. The modern environmentalist movement has already been embraced by many Christians, secularists, and adherents of other faiths. But all of us can pick up that note of reverence for the earth from the earliest forms of religious life.

Myth in Primal Religion

Primal religion also can give Christians a deeper appreciation for the importance of myth as an avenue to understanding reality. Virtually all the primal religions underscore the importance of myth. The myths are about origins of life and the community and of major phenomena. Christians cannot, or at least should not, treat myths as acceptable substitutes for a scientific explanation of observable fact. But myth, when taken as truth in story form, can be important to Christians. We repeat the story of Adam and Eve in the garden of Eden, not as fact but as a story that conveys realities about human sin and the hugely important emergence of conscience in evolutionary development. The forbidden fruit is presented as the fruit of the knowledge of good and evil. Our first reaction when exposed to the myths of primal religion should be to listen very carefully, not to reject out of hand, for truths sometimes may be found in their mythical form.

A fairly typical related aspect of primal religion is a characteristically different sense of time. The past, with its myths of origin and its ancestral spirits, is immediate, present. Past, present, and future are not a linear progression, and time is not viewed as cyclical. I'm not sure that Christians should abandon our more linear view of time. In that respect, as Thomas Cahill reminds us in the next chapter, we are deeply formed by the Hebrew view of history. And yet, there is something to be said for the immediacy of all things.

Eternity is implied, even required, by a Christian view of time. But is there not a sense in which eternity is contained in each moment of time? A great Christian hymn writer can exclaim, "Time, like an ever rolling stream, bears all who breathe away; they fly forgotten, as a dream dies at the opening day." Isaac Watts's words are true, of course. But isn't there also a deeper sense that because we are here now, it will always be that we have been? Quite apart from Christian faith in life beyond death, there is no way to erase the fact of our having lived. The immediacy of ancestors, as felt in much primal religion, conveys at least that truth. And it reminds us yet again that the way we live our lives will continue to be a reality, even after we have been forgotten.

Questions for Discussion

1. What are the similarities and differences between the modern-day environmental movement and primal religion's sense of the spiritual significance of the natural world and the interconnectedness of all life? Is it possible

to blend deeper appreciation for the natural world, as embodied in much primal religion, with twenty-first-century science and technology?

2. Why have primal religious people been more readily converted to Christianity and Islam than adherents of major religions have been to other faiths?

Chapter 3

Learning from Judaism

The Jews started it all . . . so many of the things we care about, the underlying values that make all of us, Jew and gentile, believer and atheist, tick. Without the Jews, we would see the world through different eyes, hear with different ears, even feel with different feelings.
—*Thomas Cahill*

*I*t is not so difficult to identify things Christians can learn from Judaism, because Christians, from the very beginning, *already* have learned very much from the inherited Hebrew faith.

One commentator even argues that Jews are largely, if not wholly, responsible for the basic direction of Western culture. Thomas Cahill's words above make a striking claim. He concludes that, without the Jews, "We would think with a different mind, interpret all our experience differently, draw different conclusions from the things that befall us." How could he justify such claims? Has he exaggerated what we have already learned from Judaism?

Maybe not. Cahill's basic point is that prior to Judaism, other cultures viewed history as circular. Ironically, that circular view of human existence is also found in the Old Testament book of Ecclesiastes: "What has been is what will be, and what has been done is what will be done; there is nothing new under the sun" (Eccl. 1:9). Ecclesiastes seems to say that human history has no beginning, and it will have no end. It is not going anywhere. Ultimately, there is no underlying purpose to existence. While Ecclesiastes is in the Hebrew Bible, its circular view is not the Scripture's dominant theme.

Mostly, the Hebrew story is about how God is active in human history and how our lives have purpose. Whether we can believe, with Cahill, that Judaism was unique in this sense of purpose, that it is not to be found, for example, in the Asian religions or in the Greek philosophies (which is debatable),

18

his main point should be kept in mind as we continue our journey of exploration. Cahill is certainly right in saying that Judaism presents a linear, and not only cyclical, view of human life. God has purposes, and we are invited to participate in them. That is an enormously important belief.

As far as we know, the followers of Jesus were *all* Jews; all were formed by the faith tradition embodied in the Hebrew Bible, which Christians identify as the Old Testament, and by practices common to the people of Israel in the first century CE. Jesus himself was Jewish. The vast influence of Hebrew faith on him is evident to the extent that sayings attributed to him were in fact his. Even when early Christian missionaries spread the faith throughout the Roman world, bursting the bounds of Jewish culture and practice, the faith they proclaimed was profoundly influenced by the seedbed of Judaism. When the Christian apostle Paul preached to the non-Jewish Gentiles and insisted on their inclusion in the church, there is a sense in which he represented the formula that enabled the Roman world to adopt Jewish ways of thinking about human life—as ultimately it did.

The Biblical Legacy

Much of what we call the New Testament is drawn more or less directly from the Old Testament. Sometimes such uses almost appear, to modern readers, as bordering on out-and-out plagiarism. For example, compare Luke 23:30 with Hosea 10:8, or Matthew 21:7 with Zechariah 9:9b. When the words "it has been said" appear, the allusions are to the Old Testament. Some of the sayings of Jesus are in the vein of superseding earlier commandments (as in "you have heard that it was said, . . . but I say to you"), but at other points a teaching or practice is commended as fulfilling the words of earlier Hebrew writings and commandments. And clearly all New Testament references to scripture pertain to the Old Testament. Thus, when 2 Timothy declares that "all scripture is inspired by God and is useful for teaching, for reproof, for correction, and for training in righteousness" (2 Tim. 3:16), the reference is clearly to the Old Testament. When 2 Timothy was written, there was no identifiable New Testament as scripture.

The first and greatest Christian missionary, Paul, was a carefully trained and devout Jew. After his conversion experience, he argued with Jewish leaders and insisted that non-Jews (Gentiles) could become Christian without observing various Hebrew practices; nevertheless, a serious case could be made that Paul made it possible for Gentiles to enter into what was largely a Hebrew understanding of the divine-human covenant.

So when we speak of what Christians can learn from Judaism, we begin with a huge legacy of things already learned. But what of the present situation? What can contemporary Christians learn from present-day Judaism? That is the question of this chapter.

What We Worship Is Central to Who We Are

Most of Hebrew Scripture is focused on who or what is our object of worship rather than on the philosophical question of how we can know what is true. In that sense, Hebrew religion can be contrasted with Greek and Roman systems of thought. There are exceptions to this generalization about Hebrew tradition, such as the wisdom writings of Job, Ecclesiastes, and Proverbs. But the question of worship is dominant. It is emphasized in the Ten Commandments ("You shall have no other gods before me") and in the writings of the prophets. There are some delightful parodies of the ancient polytheisms. For example:

> Their idols are like scarecrows in a cucumber field, and they cannot speak; they have to be carried, for they cannot walk. Do not be afraid of them, for they cannot do evil, nor is it in them to do good. . . . But the LORD is the true God; he is the living God and the everlasting King. (Jer. 10:5, 10a)

> To whom then will you liken God, or what likeness compare with him? An idol?—A workman casts it, and a goldsmith overlays it with gold, and casts for it silver chains. As a gift one chooses mulberry wood—wood that will not rot—then seeks out a skilled artisan to set up an image that will not topple. Have you not known? Have you not heard? . . . It is he who sits above the circle of the earth, and its inhabitants are like grasshoppers; who stretches out the heavens like a curtain, and spreads them like a tent to live in; who brings princes to naught, and makes the rulers of the earth as nothing. . . . Have you not known? Have you not heard? The LORD is the everlasting God, the Creator of the ends of the earth. (Isa. 40:18–21a, 22–23, 28a)

Those are words that Christians can also claim as their heritage, echoing the majestic cadences of early Christian creeds: "I believe in one God, the Father All Governing, creator of all things visible and invisible." We can certainly join Isaiah and Jeremiah in treating idolatry as intellectually flawed. What power do these little gods and godlets have?

So a renewed attention to this point would not lead Christians to give up on theological thought. But we do well to remember that the abstractions

typical of the thought process are not themselves life giving or life affirming. One recalls here the eloquent words of Paul that if I "understand
all mysteries and all knowledge . . . but do not have love, I am nothing"
(1 Cor. 13:2). In a Hebrew context, that love is not only interpersonal; it is
love of God.

The Theological Significance of Jesus Christ

Early on, the Hebrews thought of God as being in covenant with Israel; having, that is, a special relationship of mutual caring and mutual responsibility.
That covenant idea was very important in the development of Judaism. It
meant that the people of Israel could grow spiritually and intellectually over
the centuries without abandoning their basic spiritual foundation. Every new
insight could be seen as a new revelation about God, a new dimension in an
old relationship. In other words, the covenant with God made it possible for
people to *grow* spiritually as they came to understand God better.

The covenantal view is crucial to Christians as well, but one might suppose that the biggest difference between Christians and Jews is in their covenantal beliefs about Jesus. Christians cannot be expected to learn from Jews
that they should abandon their view of Jesus as the Christ (or Messiah), but
we may still learn something from Jewish skepticism at this point. The term
"Christ," or messiah, means "God's anointed." There is no one Jewish belief
about the coming of the messiah, but traditionally the messiah would be the
one anointed by God to bring deliverance to his people. Jews do not place
Jesus in that role. They might consider him an unusually insightful teacher
(or rabbi). Jews are skeptical about the miracle stories in the Christian New
Testament, and they do not consider Jesus to have had a uniquely superior
relationship with God.

Jewish skepticism at such points can lead Christian thinkers to more
nuanced theological views. For example, Christians often refer to the
uniqueness of Christ by speaking of the incarnation of God in Christ—that
is, God present in Christ. Here the quality of love manifested by Jesus is the
important point; this love discloses the nature of God. Christians, reflecting
on this, are challenged by Judaism to refine their understanding of the traditional doctrine of the Trinity. I will defer consideration of that until the
next chapter, "Learning from Islam," because Muslims question the centrality of Christ even more directly. But whatever else Christians may say
about the Trinity, that theological doctrine must not detract from the full
humanity of Jesus.

Attitudes toward the Material World and Human History

Another point that Christians must continue to learn from Judaism is the high value placed on the created world. The very first words of the Hebrew Bible state it clearly: "In the beginning when God created the heavens and the earth . . ." Shortly after that, it is announced that God saw that creation was good. Our Jewish roots will not allow us to regard the physical world as evil. Throughout history there have been religious tendencies to divorce spiritual life from its material setting. Some have sought to become more spiritual by rejecting the physical. Whenever such a tendency has taken form in the church, clearheaded thinkers have called us back to our Jewish roots. Christian thinkers during the second and third centuries struggled against forms of Gnosticism that denied that the material world was created by the same God who is revealed in Jesus Christ. Had the spiritualistic definition of the faith persisted, it might have led to the early demise of Christianity, because the faith would have become irrelevant to human existence.

We can also keep learning from Judaism the importance of what happens in human history, as the Cahill book has reminded us. Human life on earth is not simply a cycle of endlessly repeated events—contrary to the provocative early verses of the book of Ecclesiastes. We can have goals and seek to achieve them. The ultimate meaning of the goals is whether they are in harmony with God's purposes. God cares about what happens. To be alive spiritually is to see things as God sees them and to make God's purposes our purposes. Above all, it means pursuing justice in human society. The great prophets were alert to that, calling Israel back to its higher vision. That meant sternly criticizing injustices, even though Israel always thought of itself as the chosen people. So we have Amos declaring God's word to the Israelites: "You only have I known of all the families of the earth; therefore I will punish you for all your iniquities" (Amos 3:2). The Jewish idea of being the chosen people thus has a much deeper meaning. Israel is not chosen for special favor but for special responsibility. As a matter of fact, rabbinic writings through the centuries have been loaded with complaints to God: Why did you have to choose *us*?

What Christians Can Learn from Jewish "Chosenness"

One of the great Jewish thinkers of our time, Rabbi Arthur Hertzberg, speaks of what being a chosen people might mean after the Holocaust in which six million people were killed simply because they were Jewish. He reports the reaction of his father, a Baltimore rabbi, when he heard about the Holocaust:

When news of [the Holocaust] reached my father in Baltimore, he declared, "We should go back to Mount Sinai as a delegation and say, 'Dear God, we, your chosen people, have carried your Torah around for three thousand years. We have come now to give it back to you. We implore you, God, to. choose somebody else. Let them carry the burden.'" Of course, he did not mean what he was saying, not literally. . . . He was crying out, Why have you allowed these horrors? Why have you done this to us?

Hertzberg's own answer to why the Jews were chosen is interesting:

God expects Jews to live intensely, creatively, decently, in the moral vanguard of humankind. Chosenness is the ever-present, and inescapable, discomfort caused by conscience. . . .
The God of the Bible demands an absolute commitment to justice and compassion. That commitment is uncomfortable and burdensome. Those who live under this law must ask themselves constantly if they have done their moral duty to others. Here again, chosenness is a burden and a discomfort.

I do not know many Christians who are comfortable with the idea that Jews are the only chosen people; I know I am not. But if being chosen is expressed as responsibility, do we not have something important to learn from Judaism? If we want to think of ourselves also as chosen, is it not in that very same sense: to be chosen, not for special privilege, but for special responsibility? Protestant Christians speak of this as a vocation or calling from God. So we, too, can speak of being chosen, not only as individual Christians but as a whole church, to be God's servant in a broken world. Perhaps we can also learn to think of vocation in other institutional terms. Can a nation have a sense of vocation that transcends its own self-aggrandizement, its own narrow self-interest? What about a corporation? Does it have a vocation other than maximizing the income of its officials and investors?

The Jewish Sense of Tradition

I can think of no religion that does not embody a host of traditions. All have some sense of history, a remembrance of revered figures, repeated practices and observances of one kind or another. But if Judaism is not entirely unique in this respect, its attachment to the gathered traditions of three or more millennia is particularly noteworthy. That is partly because its traditions have enabled Judaism to sustain its being a people through millennia of history, including times of extraordinary travail. There are, of course, different interpretations of Jewish tradition within that community and different versions of how it should be expressed. One thinks of the differences among Orthodox, Conservative, and Reform Judaism, and the many subsets within these groupings. Despite the differences, many, and I believe most, Jews are resolutely committed to their traditions while *at the same time* acknowledging a deep moral commitment to the wider unity of the whole of humankind. Thus, the moral emphases evident throughout Jewish Scripture and tradition are not limited to relationships within Judaism. American Jews have often been in the forefront of social justice efforts such as the civil rights movement and other social and economic reforms.

Additionally, some Jews hold to their traditions and to Judaism's embodied ethical imperatives even if they find it difficult to believe in their theological underpinnings. It seems possible for a Jewish atheist or agnostic to remain serious in the practices of the faith. In part, this may be because one can accept the stories of one's faith in symbolic terms. A story, portrayed as literal history, may not be factual. For example, there are serious archeological reasons for believing that the traditions about Abraham, Isaac, and even Moses may be more mythical than factual. That may not matter so much if one understands that myth can convey truth that is even deeper than the factual clothing that it wears.

Many Christians tend to take the sacred stories at face value. That is true for those who insist on the literal accuracy of factual accounts, even including all the miracle stories. But it is also true among many who reject mythical accounts as unfactual, then move on without examining whether a myth, even if not factual, may embody important truth. That is remarkable, considering that we have no difficulty in being affected by truths contained in stories that make no pretense of being factually true. Most novels are prefaced with disclaimers emphasizing that any resemblance between their characters and actual people, living or dead, is entirely coincidental. The parables of Jesus, for that matter, are not offered as accounts of actual events. But we are captivated by the moral truths embodied in the parables of the Prodigal Son, the Good Samaritan, and the Servants in the Vineyard.

I write this during a Christmas season, reminded again of the incredible beauty of the stories of Jesus' birth in Matthew and Luke, reinforced by the lovely Christmas carols. The carols portray a variety of interpretations of the biblical stories, often with details specific to the location of the carols' origins, some of which are quite inconsistent with the accounts in Matthew and Luke. For instance, "In the bleak midwinter, . . . earth stood hard as iron, water like a stone," and "I saw three ships a-sailing in." The stories themselves are factually doubtful, or even inconceivable. How could a star guide the magi "until it stopped over the place where the child was" (Matt. 2:9)? Why would a census ordered by Caesar Augustus not have left any historical record, as such actions generally did? How could King Herod's alleged murdering of all Bethlehem children under the age of two have escaped any other historical notice? Not to mention the biological improbability, if not impossibility, of a virgin birth? And if, despite that, Jesus *was* born of a virgin, why is his genealogy in Matthew 1 traced through *Joseph*, the husband of Mary?

In a larger sense, these factual questions simply do not matter, if we are looking rather at the truth embodied in the stories—for instance, the tenderness and joy surrounding this birth. The emphasis on peace and goodwill. The theme of social justice expressed through the soaring rhetoric of the Magnificat of Mary, with its reversal of historic injustices—a rhetorical theme strikingly anticipated by the Song of Hannah in 1 Samuel 2:1–10. The affirmation that deep religious revelation can come to ordinary people such as the shepherds and in humble surroundings like a common stable where Jesus is depicted as being laid in a manger.

The point is that if we can set aside the factual framing of mythical stories, we are free to experience the *mythical effect*. The mythical effect occurs when the deeper truth of a myth takes hold of us and we are not unduly detained by its more superficial clothing in what may or may not be fact. This is not to say that all myths are true in this deeper sense. The myths of racial superiority inflicted on Germany during the Nazi era represented an awful distortion of the truth of our common humanity, and myths of national superiority can similarly deny that fundamental truth. But myth can convey truth, and there are beautiful illustrations of that in the Hebrew tradition. Christians can learn from that.

The Jewish Capacity to Endure

Christians can observe, almost with a sense of awe, the ability of Jews through history to endure unspeakable oppression. To be sure, Christians have suffered for their faith through persecution, but never on the scale of Jewish experience over the past two thousand years. In the past century, oppression of Jews reached demonic levels in the Holocaust when Jews were systematically murdered because Nazi Germany wanted all Jews to be eliminated. Stories of heroism survived, and some victims were able to endure and to escape to tell the story. In paying tribute to the Jewish capacity to endure, we must not believe that it is a good thing that Jews have had to endure! Would that it were possible to turn back the clock and to erase all the suffering. Still, Christians can learn something from this and other examples of endurance.

An even more compelling lesson here is that we Christians, having been complicit in the oppression of Jews, must never forget and must strive never to repeat it. Traces of this evil can be found in Christian writings. Even Christian Scriptures contain elements that have sometimes been used by Christians to justify anti-Semitism. And Christian thinkers who, in other respects, have contributed much to the positive dimensions of our faith have sometimes voiced a virulent anti-Semitism. For example, Martin Luther, primary architect of the Protestant Reformation, exemplified an anti-Jewish attitude. Hertzberg records a stunning illustration of that in this quotation from Luther:

> What then shall we Christians do with this damned, rejected race of Jews?
> . . . First, their synagogues or churches should be set on fire. . . . Secondly,
> their homes should likewise be broken down and destroyed. . . . Thirdly,
> they should be deprived of their prayerbooks and Talmud in which such
> idolatry, lies, cursing and blasphemy are taught. Fourthly, their rabbis must
> be forbidden under threat of death to teach anymore.

In these terrible words, Luther did not speak for all the Christian Reformers, and he was not even true to his own deeper insights. Philipp Melanchthon, disputing Luther's anti-Semitism, asserted that "it is always easier to accuse others when it would be better for us to indict our own." Still, Christians can learn to repent the evils that many within Christian tradition have inflicted on Jews through nearly two millennia.

I join the many Jews who deplore aspects of contemporary Israel's treatment of Palestinians and hope for a time when Israel and Palestine can dwell side by side in peace and mutual respect. But our criticism of the Israeli hardliners should be mitigated to some extent by recognition that centuries of persecution—including especially the Holocaust—have led many to a distorted quest for guaranteed security. Perhaps we can even learn something from this: only a collective security, expressed internationally, can be real under modern conditions. No nation can have full control over its own destiny.

Questions for Discussion

1. How do we square the persistence of anti-Semitism among some Christians with the fact that Jesus and his earliest disciples were Jewish?

2. What do you think of the observation that Paul's teaching was a way of drawing Gentiles in the Roman world into the Hebrew worldview? To what extent was early Christianity a departure from Hebrew tradition?
3. Is it possible to feel chosen without being exclusive?
4. Does the identification of Israel as a Jewish state add to or detract from the endurance and appeal of Judaism in the modern world?

Chapter 4

Learning from Islam

*We believe in God and that which has been revealed to us; in what
was revealed to Abraham, Ishmael, Isaac, Jacob, and the tribes; to
Moses and Jesus and the other prophets by their Lord.*
—*Qur'an 2:136*

There shall be no compulsion in religion.
—*Qur'an 2:256*

If exploring what Christians can learn from Judaism is a comparatively
easy task, perhaps the most difficult one is determining what we can learn
from Islam.

Confronting Negative Realities and Stereotypes

When we consider Islam, we must confront the realities of conflicts in the
Middle East and terrorism. Mohammad Ata and his fellow conspirators in
the 9/11 attacks prayed to Allah prior to crashing planes into the World Trade
Center and the Pentagon and a field in Pennsylvania in 2001. Suicide bomb-
ers blow themselves and others to smithereens with the assurance that they
will be rewarded in paradise. Muslim women are brutalized by the Taliban in
Afghanistan and forced to conform to rigid, discriminatory treatment based
on interpretations of Islamic Shari'a, and girls are denied access to education.
When one of my daughters-in-law was a captain in the U.S. Marines during
the Gulf War in 1991, she found that it was illegal for her or any woman to
drive a car in Saudi Arabia. (She was not amused!) In some places in the
Muslim world, apostasy or blasphemy is considered a crime punishable by
death—either by state action or by individuals responding to fatwas issued by

28

respected imams. There are passages in the Qur'an that seem to support such militancy and condemnation of unbelievers. For instance: "God loves not the unbelievers" (30:44). "Whoso desires a religion other than Islam, this shall not be accepted from him, and in the afterlife he will be among the losers" (3:84–85). "O believers, fight the unbelievers near you, and let them find you harsh, and know that God stands with the pious" (9:122).

All of that is real enough, though much depends on the translations and interpretations of the Qur'an. More to the point, such passages are balanced by recognition that Jews and Christians are generally numbered among believers, by appeals to tolerance, even treating religious diversity as God's intention, and by flatly affirming that "there is no compulsion in religion" (2:256).

Moreover, we must remind ourselves that Christian tradition and practice has its own dark side, a point we shall return to in chapter 9. We may complain about the Muslim jihad, forgetting the medieval Crusades that attempted to stamp out Islam. We think of "crusade" now as a generic term for a movement in behalf of a worthy social goal, usually by nonviolent means. We do not notice that Muslims use the term "jihad" in a similar fashion to refer to committed personal or social struggle against evil and in response to Allah's benevolent purposes. The "greater jihad" is this spiritual struggle; the "lesser jihad," which does involve defensive military action, does not imply terrorism. Meanwhile, we forget the sorry record of Christians in support of slavery, racism, oppression of women, burnings at the stake, uncritical support for national wars, and religious intolerance. Our own Scriptures contain bloody episodes, even genocides, reported with approval. And not just the Old Testament either, for the New Testament book of Revelation contemplates and celebrates a final Armageddon in which the enemies of God will be slaughtered. With some scriptural warrant, large numbers of Christians accept the proposition that unrepentant sinners will roast in hell *forever*. So we have to remind ourselves again that, in respect to Islam or any other religion, we must not compare our best with their worst. I prefer to look to the best in Islam for what Christians can learn from that faith tradition.

Muslim Openness to Others

Bearing that in mind, we discover much that is good in contemporary Islam. I am particularly struck by Muslim thinkers' efforts over recent decades to reinterpret their tradition in light of new insights and moral sensitivities. Such thinkers are engaged in what Muslims term *ijtihad*, which entails the effort to go directly to the Qur'an for fresh application and inspiration to a world that is so different from the seventh century of Muhammad. The process is not dissimilar to Christian reinterpretations of Scripture. In part, it entails decisions about what parts of a sacred writing should be emphasized and what parts should be understood as applying to a sociocultural milieu that is now past.

When non-Muslims criticize Muslims for subordinating women, they might gain a broader perspective by reading Dr. Maher Hathout's fresh Qur'anic interpretation: "The Quran granted women inheritance rights, the right to voluntarily enter into or refuse marriage, divorce rights, and the right to control their own wealth and property. . . . They were treated as legally autonomous beings, with certain economic, social and political rights. . . . Legally, both men and women enjoy equal opportunity to work, and have control over what they earn. *'Men shall have a benefit from what they earn, and women shall have a benefit from what they earn.'*" Hathout observes that "women have the right to engage in any trade, business or commercial transactions, since they are recognized as having the legal autonomy to do so."

Such words obviously do not reflect practices throughout the Muslim world. But in this and other instances, contemporary Muslim writers seek fresh interpretation of a 1,400-year-old tradition. Muslim *ijtihad* reminds us that great religious traditions change by reinterpretation more than by outright abandonment. Is this process limited to philosophers and theologians without affecting ordinary adherents of a faith tradition? I don't think so.

A personal experience brought this home to me while I was serving as a pastor in Washington, DC. After I had called on a parishioner late one night in a local hospital, I encountered two men in the darkened lobby downstairs. One of the men asked me where the chaplain's office was. I guided them there, but we discovered that the chaplain was gone for the night. The wife of one of the men was not expected to live through the night. They wanted a pastor to pray with her. I identified myself as a pastor and offered to do what I could to help. They readily agreed. Something about their manner or attire (or some other stereotype) led me to ask: you're Muslim, aren't you? Yes, they said, but that wouldn't matter. In the hallway outside the woman's room were a dozen or more friends and family. We crowded into the room. The woman, connected to life support, appeared to be nearing the end. I began by asking the direction of Mecca. With the precision of a compass, a couple of them pointed. I said I understood the importance of that to them, while reminding them that Allah (the Arabic name for God) is not limited to Mecca. God is everywhere, including in this room, and the compassionate God is here with love. So I prayed with them with thanksgiving for the life of this dying woman, acknowledging God's love and praying for family and friends gathered here in sorrow. After concluding, I commented that as a

Christian minister this was the first time I had been asked to pray with Muslims and that it had affected me deeply. I've no idea of the medical outcome. But I know that we were united spiritually that night.

Now, years later, that pastoral experience helps to underscore the religious openness of large numbers of Muslims. Of course, that openness is also evident in many Christians. But can we not gain new inspiration and hope when we see this at work in the Muslim world? Do we not learn from this that it is a serious mistake to write off more than a billion Muslims as narrow-minded fanatics?

Muslim Acceptance of Other Religions

While there certainly are Qur'anic passages that can be and often are interpreted as intolerant toward other faith traditions, a number of contemporary Muslim interpreters believe that the essential message is one of acceptance. Thus Mahmoud Ayoub writes, "I am convinced that the Prophet Muhammad and the Qur'an did not expect Jews and Christians to give up their religion and to become Muslims unless they wanted to but only to observe God's continuous care for humankind and acknowledge that the revelation he gave to the Prophet Muhammad is a genuine revelation and that Muhammad is a genuine prophet."

Such present-day Muslim interpreters cite the following reference to Jews and Christians in the Qur'an: "Those who believe (in the Qur'an), And those who follow the Jewish (scriptures), and the Christians and the Sabians,— Any who believe in Allah And the Last Day, And work righteousness, Shall have their reward With their Lord; on them Shall be no fear, nor shall they grieve" (2:62). Those words, essentially repeated in 5:69, strongly suggest that God is also revealed through Judaism and Christianity and that Jews and Christians, when they are true to their faith traditions and when they live righteously, are fully accepted by God. Ultimately, God alone will judge between differing views: "It is Thou that wilt judge between Thy Servants in those matters about which they have differed" (39:46). And "To thee We sent the Scripture in truth, confirming the scripture that came before it, and guarding it in safety" (5:48).

What, then, about passages that appear to be more intolerant? Such as: "Therefore listen not to the Unbelievers, but strive against them with the utmost strenuousness, with the (Qur'an)" (25:52). "Those who have rejected Faith and falsely rejected our Signs and the meeting of the Hereafter,—such shall be brought forth to Punishment" (30:16). "[God] loves not those who

reject Faith" (30:45). In such passages, unbelief can be understood as rejection of the truth as it is contained in the different faith traditions, not as rejection of the different faith traditions themselves. Some Muslims would still
interpret such words as referring to rejection of the Muslim religion itself—
just as some Christians reject adherents of faiths other than their own.

Christians can learn something from the broader Islamic interpretation,
accepting truths embodied in other faiths and learning from them. That is, of
course, the basic premise of this book. So we can pause here to notice that
such acceptance is not absent from Islam, not even from the Qur'an itself.
We can note also that the Qur'an contains positive references to stories and
teachings from Hebrew and Christian Scriptures. In sura 2:87, God says, "We
gave Jesus son of Mary indisputable signs and strengthened him with the
Holy Spirit." Christians who read the Qur'an for the first time are surprised
to discover that one of the suras is titled "Mary," after the mother of Jesus.

The Challenge of Islamic Monotheism

An important theological point of contention remains. It has to do with
Islam's emphatic rejection of the Christian doctrine of the Trinity, a point
that Muslims share with Judaism. That rejection is clearly stated in the
Qur'an: "Unbelievers are those that say: 'God is one of three.' There is but
one God. If they do not desist from so saying, those of them that disbelieve
shall be sternly punished" (5:73). Accompanying this is the related rejection
of the belief that Jesus is Son of God: "Those who say: 'The Lord of Mercy
has begotten a son,' preach a monstrous falsehood, at which the very heavens might crack, the earth split asunder, and the mountains crumble to dust"
(19:88). The Qur'an depicts Jesus' humility before God, renouncing every
claim to be a god worthy of worship:

> God will say: Jesus son of Mary, did you ever say to mankind: "Wor-
> ship me and my mother as gods beside God?" "Glory be to You," he will
> answer, "I could never have claimed what I have no right to. If I had ever
> said so, You would have surely known it. . . . I told them only what You
> bade me. I said serve God, my Lord and your Lord." (5:115–116)

From the very beginning, it has been hard for Muslims to see the Christian
doctrine of the Trinity as anything other than belief in three gods, *tritheism*
rather than *monotheism*. Christian rhetoric often compounds the difficulty.
For example, the theological formula defining membership in the National
Council of the Churches of Christ in the U.S.A. is faith in Christ as "God

and Savior." Christians often pray to Christ, tacitly assuming that the risen Christ can hear their prayers. Christian hymns often voice adoration of Christ in language suggesting worship. The term "Lord" can be, and often is, used interchangeably between Christ and God. Some of the New Testament passages make exalted claims concerning Christ, such as John 1 and Colossians 1:15–20.

But does the Christian doctrine of the Trinity actually refer to three gods? If so, Christianity is profoundly confused in its philosophical underpinnings. Islam (and Judaism) can help push us toward greater clarity in our language. In interpreting the doctrine of the Trinity to our Muslim and Jewish friends we can explain that the point of this doctrine is to assert the very close relationship between God and Christ: Christ was uniquely open to God, becoming in his teaching and his person a dependable avenue into understanding the nature and purposes of God. "In Christ God was reconciling the world to himself" (2 Cor. 5:19). That is not the same thing as saying that Christ *is* God; it is an understanding that God is *present in* Christ.

The classic formula of the Trinity as "God in three persons" can help. The word "person" is derived from the Latin word *persona,* for the mask worn by actors in Greco-Roman dramas to depict the character or attitude of the part being played. Suppose we were to conceive of the three persons of the Trinity as three faces or expressions of the one God. For example, God revealed in the works of creation; God revealed through the loving grace of Christ; God revealed through the loving (or holy) spirit. There is but one God, but the one God can be manifested in different ways. These faces of God are all anticipated in some depth in Hebrew Scriptures, though Christians continue to affirm the centrality of Christ as the deepest expression of the love of God.

The ambiguities often conveyed by Christian expositions of the doctrine of the Trinity can benefit from the dousing of cold water by Islamic monotheism. We have to come clean about why Christian faith is also monotheistic and not a belief in three gods.

Veneration of the Prophet

Shortly after 9/11, the Washington, DC, church I was serving reached out to the Dar Al-Hijrah Mosque in suburban Virginia. We wanted to convey our goodwill and our hope that Muslims would not be stereotyped as terrorists. With the leadership of the mosque, we arranged occasions for many of our people to meet with many of theirs. The mosque hosted us first, providing a tasty meal and an interpretation of Islam by a Muslim scholar. Then our church offered similar hospitality to the Muslims, and I had the opportunity to interpret Christianity. The theological interactions were limited and probably superficial. But the idea was to move us beyond the level of simply being nice to one another.

When it was his turn, the Muslim scholar sought to clarify the distinction between Christianity and Islam. Islam, he said, is based on the laws of God as revealed to the prophet Muhammad, while Christianity is based on the person of Jesus Christ. The prophet Muhammad is understood as the instrument through whom God has transmitted the truth. The truth is not about Muhammad himself; he is just the transmitter, the messenger. That, I thought, is a pretty accurate understanding of the difference. Muhammad received and transmitted the truth. But to the Christian, Jesus Christ, in his person, is *himself* the revelation of the truth. Law is abstraction, and abstract principle or rule is imposed from outside. Person transcends law. And yes, the Christian doctrine of love is personal, not an external abstraction. I was content to accept the contrast as the Muslim scholar had stated it.

But on further study and reflection, I found that the contrast may not be so simple. For one thing, Christians have high regard for the moral teachings of Jesus that can be framed as moral laws. And on the other hand, Muslim law constantly underscores the importance of love. Indeed, God is portrayed as the merciful one, and we are enjoined to be kind and merciful and generous to one another.

And the prophet is not simply a messenger. Muhammad is, and has been, so venerated that it is considered blasphemous to denigrate or criticize him. The veneration of Muhammad was vividly demonstrated when a Danish cartoonist caricatured Muhammad. That evoked a wave of hostility throughout the Muslim world, including a boycott of Danish goods and the issuing of fatwas by clerics calling for the death of those responsible for such blasphemy. Even more moderate Muslims, though appalled by such extremism, demonstrate great veneration and affection for Mohammad. For instance, in his liberal reinterpretation of Islamic justice, Maher Hathout always follows mention of the Prophet with the letters "pbuh"—for the classic Muslim expression "peace be upon him." Omid Safi's beautifully written *Memories of Muhammad* illustrates the spiritual appeal of the Prophet, portraying him as an inherently very good man. Safi offers illustrations of how the veneration of this man has been an important part of the appeal of Islam through the centuries. So Muhammad, to spiritually faithful Muslims, is not just a good reporter!

What can Christians learn from this? For one thing, Christians can come to value the prophet Muhammad in the same way they often appreciate other non-Christian religious figures, such as Buddha or Confucius or Gandhi.

Muhammad is different from these spiritual giants, as they are from one another. But a reappraisal of Muhammad can also lead to further enrichment of Christian perceptions of God's presence in the lives of non-Christians, despite the obvious differences. Christians may or may not be able to perceive Muhammad in this way, although I hope more Christians will.

There is also something in the Muslim view of Muhammad that may speak to Christians about the difference between venerating and worshiping Christ. It is one thing to worship God as seen through Christ; it may be another to worship the man Jesus. Muslims might even help Christians remember what happened when somebody called Jesus a good teacher. Jesus replied, "Why do you call me good? No one is good but God alone." That exchange appears in the Gospels of Mark (10:17–18) and Luke (18:18–19). Christians can continue to believe that Jesus was a very good man and that his goodness is a decisive clue to the nature of God. I certainly do. But the point is that Jesus clearly was not claiming to be God. Muslims similarly are entitled to believe that Muhammad was a very good man, and there is much evidence that he was. But Muhammad also did not claim to be God. There remains a difference between the two religious traditions, for Christians believe that God was expressed in and through Christ—not just that he accurately transmitted messages from God. But the point to be gained is that while God was expressed in and through Christ, Christ was not, himself, God.

Muslim Affirmations of the Physical World

During its earliest centuries, the Christian church struggled with the relationship between spiritual life and the physical world. Some Christians, echoing early Gnosticism, believed that their faith was entirely spiritual. The physical world, to them, was not God's creation. At best it was the work of a bumbling demigod; at worst, it was the source of evil. Spiritual life is to gain freedom from the drag of physical existence. Some went so far as to consider Christ an entirely spiritual being, to say that he only appeared to have a physical nature. This view came to be known as *docetism*—from a Greek word meaning that something only seems to be what in fact it is not. Docetism ultimately was dismissed as a heresy, and the physical world was affirmed by the church as God's creation. Still, the overly spiritual version of Christianity has often been an undercurrent in Christian life. Indeed, some aspects of physical life—particularly those having to do with sex—have been troubling to many Christians.

So we can gain something from the frank affirmation of the physical world by Muslims, as we have already seen in the discussion of what we can learn from Judaism. Far from being overly spiritualized, Muslims have even depicted heaven (and hell, for that matter) in highly physical forms. Christians may not, and I think should not, go as far as Muslims in depicting the afterlife in physical detail. But they, in common with Muslims, can affirm the physical world as God's creation.

That includes an affirmation of scientific study. In the medieval world it was largely the Muslims who advanced discoveries in science and medicine. During a time in which Christianity was a scientific backwater, the Muslims Avicenna (980–1037) and Averroes (1126–1198) were particularly noteworthy. In addition to their scientific and medicinal interests, they were respected as philosophers and theologians. Ironically, they were largely responsible for the recovery of Aristotle by Christian medieval scholastics, especially Thomas Aquinas (1225–1274), whose work was hugely influential in subsequent Roman Catholicism. Islam, almost from its very beginnings, had great respect for Greek philosophical traditions, particularly as expressed by Aristotle.

This is not to say that Islam has always been receptive to new scientific explorations nor that Christians have always neglected them. But Christianity can find its affirmations of science reinforced by the Muslim example. At their best, both Muslims and Christians have understood that honest science contributes to faith by deepening awareness of God's work of creation.

A related point can be added: Islam, at its best, has made singular contributions to art and architecture, seeking thus to illuminate the beauty implicit in God's creation. Such architectural works as the Alhambra in Spain and the Taj Mahal in India stand out as stunning illustrations. The latter also stands as tribute to a beautiful relationship between a Muslim and his beloved wife whose death consumed him with grief. Again, civilizations predominantly influenced by Christianity have also been artistically productive. But here there may also be some interreligious reinforcement.

Muslim Moral and Spiritual Disciplines

Islam has always emphasized moral and spiritual discipline. The "five pillars" of Islam exemplify this. They are (1) to affirm that "there is no god but God, and Muhammad is his messenger," (2) to fast during daylight hours throughout the month of Ramadan, (3) to pray at five specified times each day, (4) to give alms to the needy, and (5) if possible, to go on a once-in-a-lifetime pilgrimage (or *hajj*) to the sanctuary in Mecca that Muslims believe to have been built originally by Abraham. Good Muslims observe each of these five pillars, with exceptions for circumstances of real necessity. Christians do well to pay more attention to moral and spiritual disciplines, such as Lenten self-discipline.

The discipline of giving alms is strongly emphasized in the Qur'an, as it is in the Christian Bible. I cannot generalize about social welfare programs in Muslim countries, because they vary. But the basic Muslim moral attitude that it is wrong to allow people to go hungry or to want for other basic necessities easily translates into public policies in prosperous societies. There would be no place for the objectivist philosophy of an Ayn Rand that glorifies selfish individualism! Rand is celebrated by her followers for books such as *The Virtue of Selfishness* and her proclamation that she would never live for the sake of another person. Christianity, like Islam, considers selfishness to be a *vice*, not a virtue. But Christians have so often strayed from that insight. Contemporary Western culture bombards people with definitions of human fulfillment and success based on competitive greed.

The head scarves, veils, and burqas worn by Muslim women and girls have been debated and even banned in European countries, but the reasons that strict dress codes exist in Muslim culture cannot be dismissed lightly. Those reasons may be both negative and positive. Negatively, the requirement that women cover themselves can be attributed to sexism that relegates women to second-class status, utterly subordinate, first to their fathers, then to their husbands. The full burqa, concealing everything but the woman's eyes, seems a total obscuring of her individual personhood. But to their defenders, the dress codes protect women from sexual exploitation. In the burqa a woman can no longer be perceived as a sex object. She is not just a body. We can agree that women often have been subjected to sexual dehumanization, and we can gain from these cultural patterns a fresh commitment to affirm the equal personhood of women.

Some Muslim cultures have gone to extremes regarding dress codes enforced on women. For example, the Taliban of Afghanistan severely punish women for appearing in public without the burqa. That is far from showing respect for women. In fact, it is not even mandated by the Qur'an. Rather, it is an expression of conservative tribal honor-shame cultures that were patriarchal before Islam existed. Indeed, the requirement that women in some Muslim cultures wear the burqa may even be a way of holding women responsible for the sexual excesses and misbehavior of men.

In balance, it is more than doubtful that Christians will adopt anything like such dress codes—except for a handful of small sectarian groups, none of which go as far as requiring anything like the full burqa. Still, Christians can do more to emphasize that, as the saying goes, beauty is more than skin deep. European and North American societies have arguably gone too far in the other direction.

Islamic Commitment to Universal Community

Accompanying Islam's uncompromising monotheism is its always implicit and sometimes explicit universalism. God is God of all; there is a single moral universe to which we all belong. Every loyalty short of God is less than absolute, and loyalties other than to God that are treated as absolutes are idolatry. Islamic universalism is a good reminder that God is not the property of any country and that, from a religious perspective, national boundaries are secondary to God's intended universal community. Both the Muslim and Christian traditions see us as members of a single family of humankind, a reality transcending every human division. There can be none of what H. R. Niebuhr called henotheism. To be sure, nationalism is not unknown in the Muslim world. But Muslim rhetoric and practice emphasize universalism more than is typical in predominantly Christian settings.

The expression "for God and country" has often conveyed the notion that God and country have almost equal status. That is quite contrary to the universal God, as understood by Christian faith. Of course, many Christian churches and ecumenical enterprises already affirm in word and practice the universality of humankind. In one of his last letters, President Roosevelt credited Christian churches for the political support he needed for participation in the new United Nations organization. But Christians can still learn something from the Muslim emphasis on the universal.

Expressed in economic terms, universalism means that the material needs of all should be the business of all. Economic ideologies that ignore the plight of the poor fall far short of this theological vision. Muslim conceptions of economics do not always live up to that standard of moral universalism, but when laissez-faire policies hold sway over economic thought in predominantly Christian countries, we can learn something from the higher standard generally set by Muslims.

The Paradox of Medieval Islam

In her insightful study *The Ornament of the World: How Muslims, Jews, and Christians Created a Culture of Tolerance in Medieval Spain,* María Rosa Menocal tells the story of how Muslims participated in the formation of genuinely tolerant societies—especially in Spain—from the eighth to twelfth centuries. In part, this seemed to have been inspired by the Qur'anic passages affirming Judaism and Christianity that we have already noted. But it also seems to have been a broad recognition that the worship of God is not in conflict with many aspects of human culture that are not specifically religious in character. The leadership of Umayyad Muslims marked the high point in this synthesis of religion and culture as it centered in Cordoba.

The story of Muslim-Jewish-Christian coexistence from about 750 CE is complex, and the next few centuries were not without some interreligious conflict. But the broad acceptance of Arabic by people of all three religions is noteworthy, as is the early translation of Greek philosophical and literary classics into Arabic. When much of medieval Europe was bereft of intellectual resources, the libraries of Cordoba were the envy of the world.

In her summary of the significance of the cultural blendings, Menocal asks whether "the strict harmony of our cultural identities [is] a virtue to be valued above others that come from the accommodation of contradictions." She explores the long historical period "in which the three major monotheistic faiths struggled, successfully and unsuccessfully, with the question of tolerance of one another" and how this struggle occurred *within* each of the three faiths as well as among them.

Pope Gregory VII of the medieval Catholic Church joined in the mutual tolerance among Christians, Muslims, and Jews. In a letter to King Anzir of Mauretania, written in 1076, the pope used these remarkable words:

God, the Creator of all, without whom we cannot do or even think anything that is good, has inspired to your heart this act of kindness [the freeing of some prisoners]. He who enlightens all men coming into this world (John 1:9) has enlightened your mind for this purpose. Almighty God, who desires all men to be saved (1 Timothy 2:4) and none to perish is well pleased to approve in us most of all that besides loving God men love other men, and do not do to others anything they do not want to be done unto themselves. We and you must show in a special way to the other nations an example of this charity, for we believe and confess one God, although in different ways, and praise and worship Him daily as the creator of all ages and the ruler of this world.

Isn't it both fascinating and depressing that the centuries of mutual accommodation were succeeded by the terrors of the Spanish Inquisition, the expulsion of Jews and Muslims from Spain, the demonic presence of Torquemada, and of course the Crusades? The letter by Pope Gregory VII was followed but a few years later by the beginning of the Crusades, called for by a later

pope. The Spanish Inquisition was opposed by Teresa of Avila, later canon-
ized by her church. What do we learn from this? We pause over the paradox:
monotheistic tendencies toward intolerance of those outside the faith alongside monotheistic reminders that God is greater than all of us and that God's
presence can be experienced in settings far removed from our own. In our
age, when religious intolerance is expressed in most of the great religions,
we can take inspiration from the fact that during the medieval centuries Islam
cultivated a rich cultural openness. If it could happen then, as it has also in
other times and places, why not now?

Harold Bloom's appreciative foreword to the Menocal book strikes a
more pessimistic note. Citing the intolerance characteristic of several contemporary Muslim countries, he remarks that "there are no Muslim Anda-
lusians visible anywhere in the world today." Clearly the predominantly
Muslim parts of the world are in flux, with fundamentalist elements often
on display. But is it not also the case that strong democratic forces were at
work in the Arab Spring, and even more so among many Muslim leaders in
the West? The very title of Imam Feisal Abdul Rauf's book *What's Right
with Islam Is What's Right with America* makes the point, as do his comments like "a different belief system is not deemed a legitimate cause for
violence or war under Islamic law." The growth of interfaith organizations
and dialogues in many settings across America illustrate this yearning for
something akin to the rich interactions of medieval Spain. The popularity of
The Faith Club's description of how three women—a Muslim, a Christian,
and a Jew—probed and learned from each other's faith traditions over a
period of months illustrates this yearning at a different level. They remind
us that positive interactions among ordinary people can be more important,
in the long run, than dialogues among intellectuals of the different faiths—
although even the three participants in the faith club sought insights from
their intellectual traditions.

None of this is to be taken for granted. The Spanish golden age had to be
worked for by creative people of goodwill. Still, we can learn from Muslim
history that positive interaction is possible and that when it is achieved the
resulting cultural values will enrich us all.

The Mystical Side of Islam: Sufism and Rumi

Although not always identified with the mainstream of Islam, the Sufi traditions remind us that the religion has included a mystical dimension for
more than a thousand years. The poet/mystic Rumi (1207–1273) may be

the best-known example of this tradition. He is certainly the Muslim figure who is most appreciated outside Muslim circles. Was he authentically Muslim? He clearly thought so. One of his poems reads, "I am the servant of the Qur'an as long as I have life. I am the dust on the path of Muhammad, the Chosen one. If anyone quotes anything except this from my sayings, I am quit of him and outraged by these words."

Rumi's interpretation of Islam is far removed from Islamic fundamentalism or legalism. In much of his work he appears to have been remarkably accepting of others, whether Muslim or not. Majid M. Naini, a Rumi scholar, asserts, "Rumi's life and transformation provide true testimony and proof that people of all religions and backgrounds can live together in peace and harmony. Rumi's visions, words, and life teach us how to reach inner peace and happiness so we can finally stop the continual stream of hostility and hatred and achieve true global peace and harmony."

Rumi rejected religious pretension and judgmentalism, as in this quatrain from his great poetic collection, *Mathnawi:*

A conceited person sees some sin,
and the flames of Hell rise up in him.
He calls that hellish pride defense of the Religion;
he doesn't notice his own arrogant soul.

On the other hand, he recognizes the varied journeys taken by people in their quest for God:

I'm the devoted slave
of anyone who doesn't claim
to have attained dining with God
at every way station.

The great central theme of Rumi's poetry is love. Not love in the abstract, not the concept of love, but love as passionate energy. God is love, and to be alive to God is to be consumed by our love of God. The theme is illustrated in his poem "The Inner Garment of Love," which proclaims that "a soul which is not clothed / with the inner garment of Love / should be ashamed of its existence." The love of which he speaks is ecstatic. "He that is drowned in God," he writes, "wishes to be more drowned." We should not seek to "dam the torrent of ecstasy when it runs in flood." The passion of our love cannot be contained.

Rumi declares that a spirit of gratitude is more important than the things for which we are grateful: "Giving thanks for abundance / is sweeter than the abundance itself." When we become "absorbed with the Generous One," we are not to be distracted by the gift. In an expression of wonderment over the work of the creator, he writes that "everything in the universe / is a pitcher brimming with wisdom and beauty."

What can Christians learn from this version of Islamic faith? Perhaps there is little here that is not also present in the writings of Christian mystics, although Rumi's poetry is itself a fresh contribution. It is a reminder that mysticism cannot easily be contained by religious boundaries. Should all Christians strive to be mystics, in the manner of Rumi or of Christian mystics like Bernard or Catherine or Julian? Probably not, for there are doubtless temperamental factors at work in the lives of the great mystics. That said, isn't it true that most people do, at least occasionally, become passionate about their concerns? It may be only the passion of an athletic contest or a business competition or a partisan political controversy. Or, for that matter, a religious issue about which we feel threatened. Rumi and the Christian mystics at least remind us that if we're going to be passionate about anything, it ought to be about the centrality of God—and not just this or that orthodox *concept* of God—but about God as a living reality in our lives. Is this emphasis on the living reality of God in conflict with the intellectual life? Rumi sometimes seems to say so, as in his comment that "the intellectual is always showing off; / the lover is always getting lost."

Should Christians, responding to words like those, give up on the life of the mind? I have known Christians who were more than happy to consign theological thought to a forgotten bookshelf, basking instead in the glow of good feeling. Of course, that isn't exactly what Rumi is saying. Love, to him, is not just sentimentality. But the love of God remains central to our being as human beings striving for what is real in life. The apostle Paul's writings point to a view of the mind that is positive but also aware of its limitations. In a positive vein he writes, "I will pray with the spirit, but I will pray with the mind also; I will sing praise with the spirit, but I will sing praise with the mind also. . . . In church I would rather speak five words with my mind, in order to instruct others also, than ten thousand words in a tongue," referring to the emotional "speaking in tongues" in pentecostal forms of worship (1 Cor. 14:15, 19). But Paul could also write, "Has not God made foolish the wisdom of the world? For since, in the wisdom of God, the world did not know God through wisdom, God decided, through the foolishness of our proclamation, to save those who believe" (1 Cor. 1:20b–21).

Perhaps we can conclude that intellectual life devoid of spirit is empty, but spirit without thought can lose its way. Rumi is at least a reminder that a passionate love of God draws us closer to the core of what it means to be human than does thought without love.

A final point about Rumi and the Sufi movement: Its deep sense of the centrality of love resonates with much in the Asian religions we are about to explore, as it does with the other Abrahamic faiths, Judaism and Christianity. We are reminded again that any of the world religions can give rise to different interpretations, and that the Sufis draw out the most positive aspects of Islam.

Questions for Discussion

1. Is the true meaning of Islam best illustrated by Muslim extremism or by Muslim openness toward others? Which of these tendencies is most faithful to the Qur'an?
2. Does the value of the Qur'an depend on its being viewed as the literal words of God?
3. Can the prophet Muhammad be regarded by Christians in the same way as such other religious figures as Buddha, Lao-tzu, and Confucius?
4. Do you agree with the author's interpretation of the Christian doctrine of the Trinity? If not, how does one avoid the Muslim charge that Christians believe in three gods?
5. How can we learn from Muslim internationalism and Islam's affirmation of the material world?

Chapter 5

Learning from Hinduism

Hear, O children of immortal bliss!
You are born to be united with the Lord.
Follow the path of the illumined ones,
And be united with the Lord of Life.

—Shvetashvatara Upanishad

Judaism, Islam, and Christianity are sometimes grouped together as the Abrahamic faiths. That is because all three hold Abraham to be central to their earliest faith traditions. While that connection can be overstated, it is a reminder that both Christianity and Islam have been profoundly influenced by Hebrew traditions. In many respects, we are in a different religious world when we turn to the Asian religions, the earliest of which was Hinduism—acknowledging that the claim to being the oldest is disputed by the much-smaller religious group the Jains, and that some scholars say Hinduism itself is no single religious entity. Julius Lipner puts this in a striking perspective:

> Whatever else it may be, Hinduism is not a seamless system of belief in the way that many imagine or expect "isms" to be. In fact . . . Hinduism is an acceptable abbreviation for a family of culturally similar traditions. It is a family term. . . . There are many traditions over which distinctive characteristics are distributed in overlapping ways such that we may identify each of these traditions as belonging to the same cultural family.

That said, in this chapter we will seek to learn from distinctive contributions contained within that Hindu "family."

My first meaningful contact with a prominent Hindu was during seminary years at Boston University. My professor of world religions there was

Dr. Amiya Chakravarty. At that time, half a century ago, it was almost unheard of for a Christian theological seminary to have an adherent of a non-Christian religion on its faculty, and Boston University had to endure some criticism. But his presence there was a real gift to Christian students. By the mid-1950s, Dr. Chakravarty already had a distinguished career behind him. He had been a close associate and literary secretary to the Bengali poet Tagore and was well acquainted with Mohandas Gandhi and Jawaharlal Nehru. As an Indian delegate to the United Nations, he caught the attention of Boston University School of Theology, which recruited him for its faculty. For students of my generation, this was contact with Hinduism at a very high level!

After all these years I don't remember many of his specific words from the classroom. But I could never forget his spirit, unfailingly kind and generous, with never a harsh word, never a judgmental put-down of those who did not share his Hindu faith. He had participated in Gandhi's salt march of 1930, and I do recall his deep commitment to nonviolence.

He was a Gandhian, through and through. It was tempting to define all of Hinduism by the spirit of Chakravarty and Gandhi, and I fully succumbed to that temptation! In fact, I could find little there in conflict with my own Protestant Christian faith. I learned that Gandhi himself had been influenced by Christianity and that he regularly read the New Testament. Gandhi had famously declared that he was so impressed by Jesus that he could have become a Christian were it not that he did not find many Christians who were seriously committed to Jesus.

Another faculty member at Boston University during that era was a retired Methodist bishop from India, J. Waskom Pickett. Pickett had also had close associations with Gandhi, Nehru, and other Indian leaders of that formative period. While he was not Hindu himself, he underscored for impressionable seminary students like me the character of the great Mohandas Gandhi.

The picture of Hinduism that emerged from these firsthand accounts was a faith that embodied deep reverence for life, utter commitment to pacifism, and an unflinching pursuit of social justice, as expressed in the movement to free India from British colonial rule. Gandhi was widely and rightly considered to be one of the world's great spiritual leaders. If Gandhi was what Hinduism was all about, then there was much to be said for this ancient religion.

It took me quite a while to conclude that, while Gandhi was and still is hugely important as an exemplar of Hinduism, a rounded picture of this religion requires more. Hinduism is vast and complex. That very complexity is another reminder that all of the great religions and most of the smaller ones encompass a wide variety of elements. Expecting unity and clarity, we are sometimes exasperated by what appear to be inconsistencies and contradictions. Traveling through India, one is struck by the vast array of local religious practices and deities. It all seems so distant from the simplicity and depth of classroom encounter with Amiya Chakravarty!

Is it possible for Christians to learn from this religion? I believe so. Some of what we learn from Hinduism comes as reinforcement of themes we have neglected, some as points needing greater emphasis. Can we learn even from aspects of Hinduism that we reject, such as the doctrine of reincarnation or the caste system?

The Vastness of God

The first thing to be said is that God, or Brahman, is bigger than any human conception. God, in Hinduism, encompasses everything. We can be distracted by debates over whether, in Hinduism, God *is* everything, a point to which we shall return in discussing how the Selfhood (note the capital letter) of Brahman is related to our human selfhood. Hindu scriptures often deny every dualism as they emphasize the oneness of Brahman. A Hindu temple in Washington, DC, describes itself as a place dedicated to "absolute monism." God is One; there is only one God. What, then, about the references in Hindu scriptures to other gods—not to mention the shrines throughout India devoted to this or that god or goddess? Is the hint of pantheism suggested by the all-pervasive picture of the One in conflict with the polytheism suggested by references in Hindu scriptures and in the village temples? This is not an idle question, particularly where simple religious practices seem to be in conflict with the spiritual insights of Hindu teachers and writings. But ultimately the various gods and goddesses are seen as manifestations, or avatars, of the One. The one God Brahman takes different forms.

Of interest to Christians, there is a Hindu trinity, composed of three gods who are expressions of the One. In a Hindu classic, the Uddhava Gita, Brahman, represented by Krishna, is referred to as "the One who is also the three—Brahma, Vishnu, and Shiva" (24.7). Each of these expresses an aspect of the One who is Brahman. It is, however, a mistake to consider this understanding of Brahman as pantheism, for human beings retain enough freedom of the will to contribute to their individual Karma. Thus, while Brahman is all pervasive, that does not mean that Brahman causes or determines all human actions. Still, the oneness of Brahman is emphasized.

In another classic, the Bhagavad Gita, Brahman is depicted in a poetic expression of this oneness and grandeur:

The Supreme Personality of Godhead said: Yes, I will tell you of My splendorous manifestations, But only of those which are prominent, O Arjuna, for My opulence is limitless. . . . I am the beginning, the middle and the end of all beings. . . . Of lights I am the radiant sun . . . and among the Stars I am the moon. . . . Of the senses I am the mind; and in living beings I am the living Force. . . . Of the great sages I am Bhrgu; of vibrations I am the transcendental om. Of sacrifices I am the changing of the holy names, and of immovable things I am the Himalayas. . . . Of horses know Me to be Uccaibsrava, produced during the churning of the ocean for nectar. Of lordly elephants I am Airavatga, and among men I am the monarch. . . . Of weapons I am the thunderbolt. . . . Of causes for pro-creation I am Kandarpa, the god of love . . . Of purifiers I am the wind, of the wielders of weapons I am Rama, of fishes I am the shark, and of flowing rivers I am the Ganges . . . Of all creations I am the beginning and the end and also the middle. . . . Of all sciences I am the spiritual science of the self, and among logicians I am the conclusive truth. . . . I am all-devouring death, and I am the generating principle of all that is yet to be. Among women I am fame, fortune, fine speech, memory, intelligence, steadfastness and patience. . . . There is no being—moving or non-moving that can exist without Me.

Brahman, speaking through his incarnation as Krishna, summarizes this litany of his greatness by saying, "all opulent, beautiful and glorious creations spring from but a spark of My splendor."

What may Christians learn from this? Of course, it is important to move beyond preconceptions and stereotypes, such as the view that Hinduism is pantheistic. And Christians will not be comfortable with all the detail. But we should pause over the sheer *bigness* of God! It is suggestive of the Christian hymn "How Great Thou Art." But even that hymn does not quite touch the imagery of this Hindu conception. God is the ultimate source of *everything*. Most Christians affirm that. And yet, have we not a tendency to trivialize God? We speak of God as personal, and rightly so. Still, we must not domesticate God. Barthian theologians sometimes refer to God as "totally other," which is to say, completely beyond our small conceptions. That language is also misleading if it means that God has nothing to do with us. That, too, is a point where Hindu views of God do not simply depict God as absentee. But we can regain, through Hinduism, something of this sense that God is more even than words can convey. The images help. In the portion of the Bhagavad Gita quoted above, Krishna said, "With one single fraction of my Being I pervade and support the Universe."

I think it would be a good thing for Christians to understand that our God can be no smaller than the huge new perspectives unveiled by the science of recent decades. We know that the universe is not centered on the earth; in fact, the universe is trillions of times larger than this little planet. God is God of all those trillions of stars and planets out there beyond us. At the same time, God is God of the incalculably diverse forms of life on this one planet. The Hindu view of God does not treat Brahman as remote from the human drama. There are, in fact, intimate connections. And yet Brahman cannot be reduced to any one of these connections.

A deepening Christian sense of awe before God, not as fearful anxiety but as grateful reverence, can help liberate us from the idolatries that so readily infect even Christian worship itself. When worship of God is casually equated with patriotism, as in much of the God-and-country rhetoric, the vastness of God's eternal being is lost. The whole life span of any nation is no more than the blink of an eye in cosmic eternity. And when we identify any human cause, laudable as it may be, with the eternal will of God, we should pause, remembering the words Jesus reportedly spoke as he confronted death: "not my will but yours be done" (Luke 22:42). Even gratitude to God can unthinkingly imply a God that is too small. Thank God, the lone survivor of an airplane crash may exclaim. What? Does this mean that the others perished because of God's inscrutable purposes? Or another example: thank God that I just won the lottery!

Surely a view of the magnitude of God invites a profound sense of gratitude. But it must not be trivialized into seeing God as giving special favors to some while withholding gifts from others. Later, I will discuss how the awesome reality of God relates to the particular values in ordinary life.

The Hindu view of Brahman can remind us of sometimes-neglected parts of Christian tradition. For instance, we can rediscover the poetic grandeur of God as portrayed in Job 37–40, such as these words from God's speech to Job: "Have you entered into the springs of the sea, or walked in the recesses of the deep? Have the gates of death been revealed to you, or have you seen the gates of deep darkness? Have you comprehended the expanse of the earth? Declare, if you know all this" (38:16–18). Those chapters in Job are strikingly similar to Bhagavad Gita 10, quoted above. But even the awe of Job does not begin to comprehend the enormity of the universe that recent science has opened to us. Perhaps the Hindu conception of the bigness of God and the vastness of time can help us appropriate the implications of expanding scientific perceptions of the universe.

Reality and Illusion

Ultimately, in Hinduism, Brahman is the only reality. All other things that appear real are only illusion if taken in isolation from Brahman. The point is made throughout Hindu scriptures. In the Uddhava Gita, Krishna (who is an avatar or incarnation of Brahman) advises Uddhava: "Look upon this world as an illusion—a transitory creation of the mind, here today and gone tomorrow. . . . See this world for what it is: An illusion—no more substantial than a ring of fire traced by a burning torch in the dark. . . . Withdraw your attention from this world with all its appearances of forms and objects. Immerse yourself in the reality of that inner eternal bliss. Be quiet and without ambition. Then you will not be deluded." The word *maya*, translated roughly as "illusion," means something like a mirage—something that appears real but disappears the more it is examined. The challenge is to break through the illusion of this physical realm. In the *Katha Upanishad*, Nachiketa responds to Yama (another avatar of Brahman) by recognizing "that earthly treasures are transient, and never can I reach the eternal through them." So, he continues, "have I renounced all my desires for earthly treasures to win the eternal through your instruction."

In the Bhagavad Gita, Krishna tells Arjuna, "The man who sees Brahman abides in Brahman: his reason is steady, gone is his delusion. When pleasure comes he is not shaken, and when pain comes he trembles not. He is not bound by things without, and within he finds inner gladness." Krishna puts this in theological perspective: "The unwise think that I am that form of my lower nature which is seen by mortal eyes: they know not my higher nature, imperishable and supreme. For my glory is not seen by all: I am hidden by my veil of mystery; and in its delusion the world knows me not, who was never born and for ever I am. . . . All beings are born in delusion, the delusion of division which comes from desire and hate." Krishna even counsels to seek "freedom from the chains of attachments, even from a selfish attachment to one's children, wife, or home; an ever-present evenness of mind in pleasant or unpleasant events."

What are we to make of this? There are obvious difficulties in treating all aspects of ordinary experience as illusion. So we are counseled throughout these writings to act responsibly in the world. Moreover, it is asserted at many points that Brahman is in all things, providing all things their basis in reality. Perhaps the main point is that only Brahman is ultimately real. Everything else is fragmentary and time bound. All, except Brahman, are destined to pass away. So we should not be attached to the world of things in such a way that we are unable to become one with Brahman.

Most Christians would be uncomfortable with exactly that way of putting it. But isn't there an important truth in this Hindu perspective? All things do perish. Everything has a short shelf life! A Christian hymn makes the point:

Swift to its close ebbs out life's little day;
Earth's joys grow dim; its glories pass away;
Change and decay in all around I see;
O thou who changest not, abide with me.

In another verse, the hymn's writer, Henry F. Lyte, adds, "Heaven's morning breaks, and earth's vain shadows flee."

We are driven to think more deeply. Is *everything* illusion? Is everything on earth a "vain shadow"? The characteristic Hindu rhetoric about the illusory nature of everything must be modified, even in Hindu terms, by the view that everything has its being in Brahman. If the skies, the seas, the woods, the plants and animals, our physical bodies have their being as an expression of Brahman, that is not exactly to say that they are illusory. It is to say that it is an illusion to think of anything as having existence independent of Brahman. Even as expressions of Brahman they will come to an end.

We marvel at majestic mountain peaks; how permanent they seem. Yet they also will pass away, long after our short lives have ended. As I write these words, I am at our favorite retreat in the Adirondack Mountains of northern New York. Any Westerner would smile to hear these described as mountains. The loftiest of what are called "high peaks" here is Mount Marcy, topping off at a bit above 5,000 feet. Locally, it is quite a sight, though nothing like the 14,000-foot peaks of Colorado. Yet, we are told, these and other mountains of the Appalachian spine were once even higher than the Rockies. It is an illusion to think of even the greatest mountains as permanent. One is reminded of the words of Isaiah 54:10: "For the mountains may depart and the hills be removed, but my steadfast love shall not depart from you." God is permanent. Everything else will come to an end.

The Hindu take on this is that only as we find our being in God will we be liberated from the illusions of this transitory existence. As we have seen, even in Hindu terms the various expressions of Brahman can be appreciated. But attachment to these expressions is not the same as union with Brahman. As expressions, these are time bound.

Christians can go further, expressing gratitude to God for the gift of a beautiful earth and the gift of our lives upon it. I am not thinking of things to which we are attached in a selfish way, but rather of the gifts of life that enable deeper appreciation of relationships, above all our relationship with God. For instance, isn't there something about great music that draws us out of smallness and into the bigness of God? Hindus speak of Om as the eternal sound that resonates with the being of Brahman. I don't know about that. But I am tempted to think of some of the gifts of music in similar terms, hearing music as the language of the eternal. Do Beethoven's Fifth Symphony or Brahms's *Requiem* have something eternal in them, outlasting their cultural bounds? I do not know. And yet, I do not experience these gifts of creative genius as only illusion. Perhaps they are more than illusion precisely because they point toward something deep within the heart of the eternal, a view that resonates with much Hindu thought. A Hindu consultant, responding to this paragraph, has written that "the Hindu interpretation would be that such music brings us in touch with the eternal beauty of our own divinity." In any event, a reflection on the Hindu way of framing the issue can lead us toward deeper Christian insight.

Human Fulfillment

Who are we, then? How are we to find fulfillment in life? What is our final destiny? Much is made of the Hindu belief in reincarnation. That is indeed a central tenet of Hinduism, but reincarnation is not the ultimate objective. After death, in reincarnation we enter a new body, either human or lower than human, if in the present life we have not gained detachment from illusory desires. One interpretation is that we will seek out more fulfillment of unrealized desires as we enter into a new body. In the new form we are quite unconscious of previous existences, but our selfhood remains locked in the bondage of Karma—the limitations imposed by our past actions and attitudes. In the Uddhava Gita, Krishna explains that "the ignorant, who fail to distinguish the Self from its appearance as matter, get lost in the world of appearances and go from birth to death to birth again and again." They are "set on a course by the actions of a lifetime." So Krishna exhorts the seeker Uddhava to "give up this world of multiplicities experienced through the senses, and see the idea of a duality as nothing more than an illusion."

But we don't have to keep repeating the cycles of Karma. We can strive toward union with Brahman. Such union is not loss of the meaning of life; it is not the state of nonbeing. Rather, in that union we are drawn into the love of God. A passage from the *Shvetashvatara Upanishad* speaks of this:

> Hear, O children of immortal bliss!
> You are born to be united with the Lord.
> Follow the path of the illumined ones
> And be united with the Lord of Life.

Kindle the fire of kundalini deep
In meditation. Bring your mind and breath
under control. Drink deep of divine love,
And you will attain the unitive state.

Dedicate yourself to the Lord of Life,
Who is the cause of the cosmos. He will
Remove the cause of all your suffering
And free you from the bondage of karma.

We are therefore admonished to "cross over the dread sea of birth and death."

So the cycles of reincarnation are not the ultimate destiny for which we were created. Note here that the "Lord of Life" is even identified with love. The upanishad continues: "Let us adore the Lord of Life! . . . The Lord of Love is one. There is indeed no other." Such a view of God is not distant and impersonal. When one finds one's being in God rather than in transitory pleasures or accomplishments, life becomes immortal, blissful, joyful. As the *Katha Upanishad* puts it:

The joy of the spirit ever abides, but not what seems pleasant to the senses. . . . All is well for those who choose the joy of the spirit, but they miss the goal of life who prefer the pleasant. Perennial joy or passing pleasure? This is the choice one is to make always. Those who are wise recognize this, but not the ignorant. The first welcome what leads to abiding joy, though painful at the time.

The theme is voiced in the Bhagavad Gita in these words:

When the mind is resting in the stillness of the prayer of Yoga, and by the grace of the Spirit sees the Spirit and therein finds fulfillment; then the seeker knows the joy of Eternity: a vision seen by reason far beyond what senses can see. He abides therein and moves not from Truth. He has found joy and Truth, a vision for him supreme. He is therein steady; the greatest pain moves him not.

Much of this is consistent with Christian insight. How does the prayer of Augustine put it? "Thou hast made us for Thyself and our hearts are restless until they find their rest in Thee." The spiritual life is filled with joy, in contrast to transitory pleasures of this world. At this level, the Hindu contribution to Christians comes more as reinforcement than as new learning.

It is not so easy to reconcile Hindu belief in reincarnation, no matter how interpreted and qualified, with a Christian view of human destiny.

Nevertheless, we can gain something from the idea of Karma. Our actions and habitual attitudes do have lasting consequences. Hinduism does not speak of divine judgment and punishment. Its deeper insight is to help us understand that the consequences of our actions are already present in the actions themselves. Insofar as we believe that a wrathful God will consign evildoers to everlasting torment in the fires of hell, we have a hard time reconciling that with the unqualified, unmerited love of God. Still, evil actions have consequences. Even if evildoers seem prosperous and happy, the deeper spiritual reality is coarsening of the inner life. Most Christians will not be comfortable with the doctrine of reincarnation, but the doctrine of Karma that it expresses embodies important truth. I am not much persuaded by the idea of purgatory, if taken literally, but that may be a way of getting at the same point as the Hindu reincarnation: a period of purging oneself of the sinful habits acquired through a life of wickedness.

The Hindu emphasis on union with Brahman through detachment from the illusions of this world would seem to lead directly toward asceticism, combined with rigorous disciplines of meditation. That is indeed a Hindu emphasis. But it is a mistake to consider this an otherworldly abandonment of responsibilities in this world. Difficult as it may be to reconcile the teaching about Brahman as the only reality and our attachment to things of this world as illusion with teaching about responsibility, that tension must be preserved. A deeply committed Hindu friend, in informal conversation, speaks of the meaning of illusion as "a much-misunderstood aspect of our philosophy— regrettably, even by many Hindus." He continues:

> The fundamental truth is that there is nothing at all separate from Brahman; the diversity that we see is only an appearance of difference. It is superficial, not substantive. Even knowing this, we must deal in the transactional world fully cognizant of differences that we perceive. Declaring the world to be an "illusion" and copping out of our responsibilities to others is hypocritical. A prior step is to recognize that our own body, mind, and personality is itself an "illusion," which requires that we stop pampering ourselves, catering to our own comfort and convenience.
>
> Those not willing to do so, have no business to step back from duties as spelled out in our "Dharma." On the other hand, those who live this knowledge will act spontaneously in harmony with nature without any selfish agenda or sense of personal accomplishment.

This perspective, from Dr. D. C. Rao, reminds Christians that their faith in God cannot be an escape from responsibilities in this world. Christian history, which includes occasional escapes into asceticism or withdrawal in anticipation of Christ's imminent return and the end of the world, provides some examples of irresponsibility. Even worse is the more common hypocrisy of those who cover their self-centered materialism with a veneer of otherworldly Christian rhetoric. Not infrequently, a parishioner who has been annoyed by a prophetic sermon will accuse the preacher of mixing religion with politics or materialism. The gospel is "spiritual," and not material—say people whose lives demonstrate much more materialism than spirituality. Many of the great Christian mystics—such as Bernard of Clairvaux and Catherine of Siena—were profoundly engaged with the worldly issues and problems of their age. Catherine ministered among victims of highly communicable disease, undermining her fragile health. Meanwhile, she communicated with popes and kings about their responsibilities to the poor. Could one not say similar things about the great twentieth-century Hindu saint Mohandas Gandhi? Hindu writings help us think more rigorously about this combination of devotion to God and moral responsibility.

The *Taittiriya Upanishad* contains especially clear moral appeals. For instance, "Wisdom means a life of selfless service." And:

> Waste not food, waste not water, waste not fire; fire and water exist to serve the Self [Brahman]. Those who realize the Self within the heart stand firm, grow rich, gather a family around them, and receive the love of all. Increase food. The earth can yield much more. . . . Refuse not food to those who are hungry. When you feed the hungry, you serve the Lord, from whom is born every living creature. . . . Realizing this makes . . . our feet ready to go to the help of everyone in need. Realizing this we see the Lord of Love in beast and bird, in starlight and in joy, in sex energy and in the grateful rain, in everything the universe contains.

In the Bhagavad Gita, Krishna says that "those who set their hearts on me and ever in love worship me, and who have unshakeable faith, these I hold as the best Yogis." These are people "who have all the powers of their soul in harmony, and the same loving mind for all; who find joy in the good of all beings." And "only by love can men see me, and know me, and come unto me." Such love extends even to enemies as much as to friends. Such a person is not affected by "honour or disgrace, who is beyond heat or cold or pleasure or pain."

So Hinduism does not foster a passive attitude toward life. As the Bhagavad Gita puts it, "Not by refraining from action does man attain freedom from action. Not by mere renunciation does he attain supreme perfection. . . . Action is greater than inaction: perform therefore thy task in life. Even the life of the body could not be if there were no action."

Life Stages and Personality Differences

An aspect of this is worth further thought. Some of the Hindu scriptures speak of different stages of life in which people can be expected to relate to God and the world in different ways. For instance, during one's early years, one is a student, learning about life and the formative traditions that are the inherited legacy of past wisdom. Then in the middle years, one is a householder, married and with family and other responsibilities. Later, one is retired from active duties, free to explore the ultimate meaning of life more fully. Still later, the goal is to reach the state of union with God and freedom from the illusions of temporal existence. No matter what stage of life one is in, the ultimate reality is one's being in God.

But a striking aspect of typical Hindu thought is its nonjudgmental attitude toward the attachments people typically have with objects of desire. Early on, a person may seek fulfillment through sensual gratifications. That is, to Hindu thought, an aspect of human existence that is entirely to be expected. In time, however, one becomes sated with such gratifications, yearning for something more. That something more can be expressed in social status: power, wealth, prestige. This, too, is to be expected. But these goals, once achieved and lived with long enough, also fail to satisfy. One may then come to the point of renouncing such things. But renouncing illusory goals is not, in itself, union with God. Finally, perhaps after many rebirths, one may come to the ultimate union which, alone, brings fulfillment.

Implicit in this nonjudgmental attitude is recognition that it does no good to repress human desires. A repressed desire remains. It is not felt as an illusion that is no longer attractive; rather, it is a craving or a yearning that must be resisted by force of will. When such desires are condemned by society or religious tradition, one represses them in order to be more acceptable to others or to the unseen God whose approval is important. But the desire, the craving, the yearning remains.

So this Hindu reluctance to judge could be described as recognition that the desires are simply immaturities out of which one can grow when their inability to satisfy becomes evident. That does not mean that truly harmful behaviors should be condoned. The Holocaust was not simply an expression of immaturity!

Even presented in such a simplified form, the Hindu view may have some insight to offer Christians. It can at least remind us that human desires and yearnings cannot finally bring fulfillment apart from a desire to be in loving relationship with God and fellow humanity. Only a life of love is ultimately fulfilling.

Further, the Hindu perspective is that people will experience different ways of progressing toward union with God. Some are more intellectual in their approach to life. Some are more emotional. Some are more active. We all have minds and hearts and wills, but Hindus recognize that not all people are the same. Different ways of seeking union with God can be equally productive. In harmony with this view, Hindu thought has generally been open to different religions. There is no need to convert Christians or Muslims to Hinduism, and by the same token, efforts to convert Hindus to other religions are rejected.

Christianity and Islam are both evangelistic faiths. At best, they seek to share the heart of their faith with nonbelievers and to draw them into the institutional expressions of that faith, in church and mosque. Given all the effort poured into institutional evangelism, the results, historically, have been meager. Converts are often those who have been abused or disrespected or at least neglected in their original religious settings. In India, for instance, the untouchables have been most receptive to conversion to Christianity. In America, African American prison populations, typically neglected and stigmatized by church people, have proved to be a fertile field for Muslim missionary activity.

The Caste System

Part of a responsible life is acting in ways appropriate to one's social location (to use a term borrowed from Western sociology). The caste system, by which this is largely framed, is much maligned by Christians—and often for good reasons. But it is also questioned by serious Hindus.

Hindu scriptures recognize diversity of social classes and human temperaments as an aspect of all societies. But the Hindu term *Varna*, sometimes mistakenly understood as "caste," refers to four basic types of temperament that lead to four social classes: Brahmins (not to be confused with Brahman), who are priests and teachers; Kshatriyas, who are rulers and protectors; Vaishyas, who are merchants and traders; and Shudras, who are peasants and artisans. All have important roles to play in the well-being of society; none should despise the others. Nor is Varna inherited from parents. It is more the inheritance of previous incarnations. Doing one's work in the context of one's Varna is not the same as opening oneself up to Brahman, but it is not inconsistent with progress toward the union with Brahman, the ultimate unitive state. Moreover, people in the different Varnas have no basis for feeling or acting superior to any others.

The caste system must not be confused with Varna. The caste system is a social construction, common to Indian society but in many respects fundamentally opposed to the basic Hindu concept. That is especially evident in the treatment of outcastes, the Dalits. Gandhi, who believed in the social categories represented by Varna, was especially and resolutely opposed to categorizing any as outcastes, the so-called untouchables. These Dalits are thoroughly dehumanized. Their function in society is to do the dirtiest, most menial jobs that nobody else would touch. They are called untouchable because the slightest touch of a Dalit by members of the other castes creates feelings of aversion, even uncleanness. The stigma of untouchability persists to some extent despite the efforts of people like Gandhi and its being outlawed in contemporary India. But the division of roles can be discussed apart from any connection with the now largely discredited consigning of millions to outcaste status or to other rigidities in caste structure. India has made considerable progress in eliminating this odious form of discrimination. That progress was best symbolized by a Dalit, K. R. Narayanan, becoming president of India.

I am struck by two references in the Upanishads that question the ultimate reality of caste. One of these, in the *Brihad-Aranyaka Upanishad*, says that in the unitive state—when one is united with Brahman—"there is neither thief nor slayer, neither low caste nor high, neither monk nor ascetic." The other, in the *Mundaka Upanishad*, reminds the seeking Hindu that "the deathless self has neither caste nor race." Still, social division remains a Hindu reality, and some Hindu scriptures say that emphatically. In the Uddhava Gita we read that "those who live outside a Varna will tend towards a lack of faith. They will become dishonest in their dealings—stealing and quarreling needlessly. Impurity, anger and desire will be the characteristics of those outside the varnashrama system." By contrast, those within the system will be marked by "non-violence, truthfulness and honesty, freedom from desire, anger and greed, always seeking the happiness and well-being of all." Clearly there would be no place for Dalits, or outcastes, in this concern about the "happiness and well-being of all"! But the Varna system, as such, seems well established in Hindu teaching, and the caste system persists in Indian society.

Given the strong Hindu affirmations of reverence for life and practice of nonviolence, it may seem remarkable that a person whose responsibilities include maintenance of order and protection of the people can engage in military practices. The classic Bhagavad Gita is partly framed around this military responsibility. The Gita tells the story of an interaction between Krishna (the avatar or incarnation of Vishnu and ultimately an expression of Brahman) and the warrior Prince Arjuna. A battle is about to occur in a dispute over royal succession. Arjuna, a brave and outstanding warrior, is deeply concerned about friends and relatives on the other side whom he does not wish to kill. But Krishna urges him on. It is his duty. And besides, those slain in battle will move to a new reincarnation. Thus, "when a man sees that the God in himself is the same God in all that is, he hurts not himself by hurting others: then he goes indeed to the highest path."

So it is possible, even in the exercise of violence, to be in harmony with God. Later, Krishna lists nonviolence, along with a litany of other moral qualities, as "treasures of the man who is born for heaven." The list is worth repeating here as evidence of the moral underpinnings associated with those who are attuned to God: "freedom from fear, purity of heart, constancy in sacred learning and contemplation, generosity, self-harmony, adoration, study of the scriptures, austerity, righteousness; non-violence, truth, freedom from anger, renunciation, serenity, aversion to fault-finding, sympathy for all beings, peace from greedy cravings, gentleness, modesty, steadiness; energy, forgiveness, fortitude, purity, a good will, freedom from pride." Such qualities, pursued while one is responsibly attending to the work of one's caste, prevent one from treating caste as a mark of status.

What can Christians learn from this portrait of the Hindu Varna system? A negative learning is that every social system is vulnerable to the idolatries of status and the dehumanization created by social divisions. That is especially evident in the oppression of outcastes. Even among the four traditional Varnas and their subcategories, pride of status is a persistent reality among many in India. Christians, particularly in America, still live with the legacy of a racial caste system in which African slaves and their descendants lived in a cultural setting not unlike that of the Indian outcastes. While social roles in America are not as rigidly defined as the Indian caste system, Christians do well to heed the Hindu message that whatever our social roles, our deeper life belongs to God and our social role should be defined by the service we can render to others.

Paul did not apply his wonderful metaphor of different roles within the church as the "body of Christ" to responsibilities in the wider society. But the metaphor also fits beautifully there. If we think of the wider society as a body containing many members who must live in cooperation with one another, like the cooperation of different parts of the human body, then we can help to heal the tragic brokenness of most human society. Could the CEO of a Fortune 500 company see him- or herself as a fellow worker with a computer technician or a janitor? Could the material rewards of different kinds of work be distributed more equitably? In the early years of the twenty-first century, inequality of wealth and income has expanded geometrically. In the political realm, could a senator or governor or president view the office not as a status possession but as an opportunity for service—and have the political courage to sacrifice the office if necessary for the well-being of society? Here, too, in the early twenty-first century we are more often treated to the spectacle of politicians who will do almost anything—including using attack ads that debase the culture—to win elections.

These are not idle questions. I am very far from urging Christians to accept anything like the Indian caste system, nor am I advocating absolute equality in the social reward system. But the cooperative sense that is implicit in the basic concept is worth pondering.

Moreover, while the rigidities of caste are to be deplored, the job security implied by such a system is not unimportant. At the very least, a person's willingness to work must be matched by society's commitment to provide work that is to be done. Unemployment is not only an economic problem, it also is a serious moral breakdown.

Hindu Beliefs about Evil

Every religion has to face the problem of evil, if evil is defined as the defeat or frustration of the good. However it is viewed, evil is in direct contrast with good. Illustrations leap to mind: Young boys in West Africa, drugged and conscripted into militia units, trained to cut off the limbs of other children. Young girls drawn into a life of prostitution, sometimes as the sole visible way to escape poverty. Hundreds of thousands of refugees in drought-stricken and war-torn regions who are dependent on international aid, the arrival of which is prevented by warlords. Babies with bloated stomachs who will die of starvation if epidemic disease does not kill them first. A Ponzi scheme through which a shrewd financier bilks people of their life savings, thereby accumulating billions for himself. A serial killer who murders random victims over a period of years. Anybody could add dozens of other illustrations from recent news reports. Such cases represent conscious, intentional decisions by individuals or groups or even nations, mostly for selfish reasons, without the slightest regard for the good that is diminished or destroyed. Topping the list of twentieth-century evils is the Holocaust in which more than six million Jews were slaughtered, the massive intended starvation of millions of Ukrainian Kulaks and the starvation of many millions in China, and other instances of genocide.

But one also thinks of natural catastrophes: tsunamis, hurricanes, floods, tornadoes, forest fires. Tornadoes that swept across the American South in

2011 and 2012, along with floods in that period, killed and injured people and left thousands of people homeless. While such disasters are not a result of anyone's malevolent actions, the consequences clearly frustrate the good in the victims' lives. Often disasters of this kind are called natural evils. Whether it results from human wickedness or the vagaries of nature, human tragedy forces religion to frame a response.

What can be learned from the Hindu understanding of evil? Begin with the surprising Hindu teaching that evil is an illusion. In dialogue 14 of the Uddhava Gita, Krishna instructs Uddhava: "What are the definitions of good and evil? Judging another to be good or bad is evil. To cease making judgments between good and bad, that is true goodness." In dialogue 23, Krishna asks, "What is real and what is unreal? What is good and what is bad?" Yet, he continues, "making such judgments and speaking about them gives them a reality in one's mind." He reminds Uddhava that "this world of experience does not exist any more than a dream does."

The Hindu attitude toward evil is well summarized by my thoughtful Hindu friend D. C. Rao:

> In our tradition there is really no such thing as "evil" in the sense of an independent force causing people to do "evil" or "sinful" things. It is only our ignorance that leads us to do things that are not in our own long-term interest. It is these actions born of our ignorance that we regard as "sinful." As long as we are ignorant, we are bound to be reborn again and again until we start the journey toward knowing our true nature, i.e., eternal consciousness, bliss. We do not escape this cycle by merely "doing good." That is not enough. Leading an ethical, moral life is a necessary but not sufficient condition for liberation. Liberation comes from removing the ignorance of our true nature that can itself happen through reflection or from ardent devotion to God.

Reflecting on such statements about evil, the reader may notice a paradox. Evil does not exist, and yet throughout Hindu scriptures there are exhortations to do good and warnings about what to avoid. That is to say, there seems to be a clear sense that there are behaviors and attitudes that impede our progress toward human fulfillment in union with Brahman and perpetuate our bondage to the endless cycles of reincarnation. One colorful reminder of this is in dialogue 22 of the Uddhava Gita when God, speaking through Krishna, asserts, "Anyone who steals that which is meant for worship—even if it was a gift that the thief originally made—such a one will live as a worm for ten thousand times ten thousand years." Evidently evil by any other name is still evil!

Still, a Christian can learn something from the Hindu idea that the *basis* of evil is illusion. Evil, to the Hindu, does not have an independent existence. There is no room for a devil figure coexistent with God. When human beings do evil things, it is generally because they mistakenly believe that is the best way for them to achieve human fulfillment. We cannot know the inner mind of Adolf Hitler or Osama bin Laden, but isn't it likely that these personifications of evil in recent history—along with countless others whose wickedness is not so publicly visible—were captivated by an utterly false conception of human reality? To have more power—or wealth, or prestige—than anybody else might seem to make one more human. To the Hindu, these human goals are illusions. Power, wealth, and prestige are ultimately empty. That understanding is also deeply rooted in Christian tradition. But Christians have been much more inclined than Hindus to personify evil, granting it an unreal status.

The problem of natural evil—the bad things that happen to people as a result of natural forces like tornadoes and earthquakes—may be more complicated. Such events occur regardless of our actions. Sometimes these are referred to as acts of God, implying that the inscrutable will of God has chosen to make people suffer. In legal documents, "act of God" just means that something has happened that people could not prevent. To believe that God has *chosen* to cause pain and sorrow to some, while sparing others, requires a degree of determinism that many Christians (myself included) find unacceptable.

Most natural catastrophes can be explained in natural terms, and scientific studies continue to refine human understandings. Of course, human actions in preventing damage, or at least getting out of the way, do affect what happens to us. Today we study the effect of human actions on global warming. Building homes in areas prone to flooding and erecting buildings that cannot withstand earthquakes are, if not morally culpable, at least foolish. I recall, with wonderment, the sight of many houses on the lower slopes of Mount Vesuvius, a volcano that has erupted with some regularity for many centuries. The people of ancient Pompeii could be excused for not expecting what happened to them, but we should know better now!

A Hindu perspective on what we call natural evil can maintain that our experience of this as evil is an illusion. But, as we have seen, Hindus remain committed to responsible action. An attitude of taking all suffering in stride is also consistent with Christian faith in the love of God to sustain us, no matter what happens. The notion that God suffers with us may be more uniquely Christian.

Conclusion

I can see why the Hindu saint Mohandas Gandhi was attracted to the New Testament and much Christian moral teaching, even as he remained a deeply committed Hindu. As we have seen, there are notable parallels of spiritual insight. At some points, Hindu teaching can reinforce Christian commitments. At other points, Christians can gain greater insight into their own faith by reflecting more deeply on Hindu perspectives. Substantial differences remain. Careful study of Hindu scriptures and practices can at least keep us from caricatures of this vast and ancient religious tradition.

Questions for Discussion

1. If we cannot know *everything* about God, how can we be sure we know *anything* about God?
2. When Hindus refer to Jesus as an avatar, or manifestation of God, how does this differ from Christian understandings about Christ?
3. If we, like Hindus, recognize that spiritual life necessarily advances through stages, will that lead us to be too complacent about sin and evil? How should we draw the line between tolerance of moral and spiritual immaturities and deeply destructive attitudes and behaviors?
4. Do differences of caste, corresponding to different temperaments and capabilities, necessarily lead to divisions based on higher and lower status? Can such differences lead to a deepened sense of mutual responsibility rather than heightened competitiveness?

Chapter 6

Learning from Buddhism

Buddhism has enabled me to make sense of my Christian faith. . . .
Without Buddha I could not be a Christian.
> —Paul F. Knitter

*D*espite important similarities, Buddhism is not simply a subset of Hinduism. Historically, Buddhism did arise in the same cultural context. But in some respects it can be regarded as a reaction against aspects of that context. It is an ancient faith, dating from the sixth century BCE.

There has been a resurgence of interest in Buddhism in Western countries in recent years. Some Christians have found it possible to combine aspects of Buddhist teachings with their own faith traditions, without abandoning Christianity as their primary religious home. An advance reader of this chapter speaks of her avid reading of Buddhist books for the past fifteen years. She writes, "In my years of studying Buddhist thought, I have become a better Christian. I am more capable of loving my neighbor, myself, and more capable of feeling gratitude for the mystery of the world and of my precious birth." This chapter may not have such an outcome for all readers, but I hope to illustrate that Christians do have things to learn from Buddhism.

Buddhist Tolerance

Buddhism has a general reputation for being a tolerant religion, perhaps the most tolerant of the great world religions. There have been instances of Buddhist participation in sacred violence and religious forms of nationalism, including support of oppressive regimes. But there is not much in its history like the Inquisition or the Crusades or more recent forms of Christian intolerance—or like suicide bombings by Muslim fanatics.

Buddhist openness was brought home to me while I was serving a United Methodist church in downtown Washington, DC. A young Cambodian Christian friend contacted me early one week to ask me to baptize his infant son. It needed to be done quickly because this father had just learned that he had to be in Cambodia by the following Saturday for a unique career opportunity. So the baptism couldn't occur during the next Sunday's church services, as would have been our normal practice. Instead, we would do it at the midweek Communion and healing service in our small chapel. The infant's mother was Buddhist, but she was willing to participate in the prebaptismal counseling and even to take the vows along with her husband. She also invited a number of Cambodian friends, most of whom were clearly Buddhist. They included an elderly patriarchal figure who arrived at the chapel dressed in traditional Cambodian attire.

After the baptism, it was time for the Communion service. With more than a dozen Buddhists on hand, I carefully explained what the Christian rite was all about. I found it refreshing to tell the story of the Last Supper of Jesus to people who had never heard it before. When it was time for people to commune, I said that all are welcome, though nobody is required to participate. I suspected the Buddhists would not feel that they could. To my surprise, the first one to stand and lead his fellow Buddhists forward was the elderly patriarch. He knelt at the altar rail with great dignity, communing with obvious respect for this Christian rite. Some Christians might object. But in the Gospel accounts, Jesus freely gave the bread and wine to everyone, including Judas Iscariot, who was to betray him that very night. If Judas could be given Communion, how could I refuse these respectful Buddhists? I've no idea what effect this might have had on them, although refusal on my part would surely have come across as rejection—quite contrary to the core meaning of this central Christian sacrament.

I found the openness of the Buddhists to their Christian sisters and brothers deeply moving. Perhaps we could learn something from that. But there are other, more complex points we also can learn from Buddhists.

Some Background

Like each of the other major world religions, Buddhism is an incredibly complex religious movement. There are very different branches and interpretations—and Buddhism, as we have noted, has been around for a very long time. We cannot linger over the whole history, but a few facts help to set the stage. Buddhism emerged in India as a distinctive variation of what would later be central tenets of the classical Hindu worldview, a religion discussed in chapter 5. The person we know as the Buddha was Siddhārtha Gautama, born in 563 BCE in a royal family. A young man of extraordinary grace and promise, he seemed destined to become an unusually fine ruler. He married at age 16. His wife bore him a son. He was granted every privilege in life, and his father, in particular, sought to protect him from any view of suffering and death. Despite this, while riding outside the palace, he came face-to-face with grim human realities. He encountered first an ugly, decrepit old man, and then a very sick man, and then a dead man being carried by, and then a wandering ascetic. He asked his driver the meaning of the suffering and death. He was told, "This comes to all men."

Profoundly shaken by such realities, the young Gautama left his home in search of enlightenment. He exchanged his princely robes for the rags of a beggar. Seeking out sages, he found no answer. He tried self-denying asceticism for several years—still no answer. Then, while he was seated under the bo tree for seven days, his moment of enlightenment finally came as a profound understanding of the root causes of suffering and death and the way to Nirvana. Rather than entering into the blessedness of the state of Nirvana, he turned back to the world with compassion for all who suffer so that he could offer enlightenment and liberation. Over the next forty years he taught and led an increasing number of monks who followed him and, in turn, influenced others. In the centuries following his death, the movement spread to other countries, becoming the dominant religion in several. Today it is difficult to know how many Buddhists are in the world, but the number is clearly in the hundreds of millions.

The influence of Buddhism extends well beyond the number of committed Buddhists. Buddhist teachings and practices of spiritual discipline have proved useful to many adherents of other faiths. That is illustrated by Paul Knitter's book *Without Buddha I Could Not Be a Christian*. After surveying key Buddhist teachings that he has found persuasive, he concludes that although Christ remains primary to him, "I suspect (though I am not sure) that what I have discovered in my process of Christian–Buddhist double-belonging characterizes many if not most other double-belongers: there is a core religious identity (which is often the tradition one grew up in) that enters into a hybrid relationship with another religious identity and tradition. . . . Even though my primary allegiance is to Christ and the gospel, my Christian experience and beliefs have not dominated nor always had to trump what I learned or experienced through Buddha."

We cannot here survey the whole Buddhist picture, of course. But the question remains: Can Christians learn from this faith?

I put that question to a leading Buddhist minister a number of years ago. He had been my student in California in the 1960s, but now we were both members of the national board of the Interfaith Alliance. I told him I was going to be dealing with that question in a sermon and asked him, as a Buddhist, what main things he would say that Christians could learn from Buddhism. He threw up his hands—there is just too much. A Christian cannot grasp Buddhism, he exclaimed, without much more study. Limited knowledge can even be dangerous. I persisted. Isn't it true that our knowledge is always going to be limited? Did not even the Buddha himself have limited knowledge? Yes, he smiled. And perhaps he could even appreciate what I was doing, limitations and all, as an expression of my "Christian karma"! So what could a Christian learn? My friend observed the difference between the ways in which Buddha and Christ are portrayed, in pictures or statues. Christ is shown with great passion, with sweat and blood, as on the cross. Buddha is never pictured as passionate: always serene, never flappable, the wise one. Passion versus the renunciation of passion: is that what it comes down to?

Before getting to that, we have to remind ourselves that Buddhism reinforces a great deal of Christian teaching. Some of the little samplings of Buddhist ethics could almost appear in the New Testament's Sermon on the Mount. For instance,

All we are is the result of what we have thought: it is founded on our thoughts and made up of our thoughts. If a man speaks or acts with an evil thought, suffering follows him as a wheel follows the hoof of the beast that draws the cart. . . . Hatred does not cease by hatred; hatred ceases only by love. That is the eternal law. . . . The wise man will not look for the Faults of others, nor for what they have done or left undone, but will look rather to his own misdeeds. . . . Let us live happily without hating those who hate us. Let us be free from hatred among those who hate.

Can Christians learn from that? That is already pretty good Christian teaching. Perhaps we can learn that those ideas from the New Testament speak to something universal in human experience. They are not isolated in our own Western Christian traditions. Much more of Buddhism is like that.

Buddhist Atheism

What about the more fundamental faith in the reality of God? Is Buddhism atheistic? If so, what can we possibly learn from that?

Sometimes Buddhism is characterized as the only major world religion that does not believe in God. That is vigorously debated, both within and beyond the Buddhist community; it may partly come down to matters of definition. It is beyond my purpose here to try to resolve the debate. It is certainly true that many, if not most, Buddhists avoid talking about God. In a sense God-talk is considered by Buddhist thinkers as changing the subject from what we should be talking about. To focus our attention on God as center and source of all being is to be distracted from the primary task of life.

Our central purpose is to achieve enlightenment, a process requiring great concentration and progressive freedom from the distractions and illusions that constantly prey on us. What is enlightenment? Central to Buddhism is the belief that enlightenment cannot be conveyed in words. It cannot be described. You, like Buddha himself, will know it when you have it! Its fruits, its effects will then be evident to you and to others. In the most sublime sense of the word, you will have become a truly spiritual being. Even those of us who are not Buddhists can recognize something of that spiritual quality in historical figures like the Buddha himself and contemporary Buddhists like the Tibetan Dalai Lama.

Those of us who can lay no claim on being enlightened in the Buddhist sense may still ask whether this avoidance of talking about God has anything to say to people for whom God is so central. Perhaps it can at least mean this: Talk *about* God runs the risk of turning the reality of God into an abstraction. When the *word* "God" or the *idea* or *concept* of God replaces the living reality, then not only have we lost something of our own spiritual foundations, but we also have departed from the core meaning of Christian faith itself. That is so easy to do. The historic Christian creeds point to that core meaning, but they necessarily do so with words. When adherence to those words and the theological formulas they convey is taken to be the true test of faith, defining who belongs and who does not, distinguishing between persons who are orthodox and those who are heretics, then the *reality* of God can be lost. The fact that Buddhists don't insist on such creedal orthodoxy may be one reason that they haven't burned people at the stake as heretics! What does that say to Christians whose historical traditions include many instances of cruel repression?

Christians will not abandon belief in God. But perhaps from their Buddhist friends they can learn something about how *not* to believe in God. It is the reality of the living God that counts, not the abstraction. To be sure, theology matters. It points in certain directions and away from others. Even the concept of heresy has a place. For example, the racist belief that certain physiological factors, such as skin color, are marks of human superiority or inferiority needs to be identified and warned against. Still, our emphasis should be more on affirming the realities that we consider to be true than on condemning what we believe to be untrue. Perhaps it is time for us to move beyond the sorry history of heresy trials and anathemas.

Moreover, Christians can be reminded by Buddhists that in the cultivation of our own spiritual life, it is the reality that matters most—not the correctness of our concepts. The late Christian theologian Paul Tillich made this point in a Harvard classroom many years ago. A student asked him to comment on "the prayer life of a theologian." "Well," he said, "the theologian must pray twice as much as anybody else." Why? He didn't elaborate. But perhaps he was acknowledging that theologians (including himself) necessarily spend so much time on concepts that they can come to regard the ideas about God and other aspects of faith as the reality. God has been turned into an object. In prayer, however, one opens oneself to the living reality without rigid preconceptions.

Religious Authority

Buddhism has no pope nor authoritative bishops. Throughout its history, beginning with the Buddha himself, certain figures have been very influential. Buddha, of course, heads the list. Still, Buddha emphasized to his disciples that they should not just take his word for anything but should test its truth with their reasoning minds. The Dalai Lama, considered by many to be the most influential Buddhist leader in the contemporary world, makes the point: "Do not take the Buddha's words literally simply out of reverence. Examine them and respect them only when you have seen a good reason for doing so." Even beyond this, it is said that when a novice refers reverently to Buddha, some Zen Buddhist masters will explode with a wholly unexpected rebuke. In his classic study *The World's Religions*, Huston Smith reports on the approach of Zen Buddhist masters:

> A master, Gutei, whenever he was asked the meaning of Zen, lifted his index finger. That was all. Another kicked a ball. Still another slapped the inquirer.
> A novice who makes a respectful allusion to the Buddha is ordered to rinse his mouth out and never utter that dirty word again. . . .
> A monk approaches a master saying, "I have just come to this monastery. Would you kindly give me some instruction?" The master asks, "Have you eaten your breakfast yet?" "I have." "Then go wash your bowls."

The Zen masters' point is that true enlightenment goes beyond veneration of Buddha. I do not wish to push this too far, but perhaps Christians can learn something of the sheer *transcendence* of ultimate reality and the need to be more attentive to the immediate life about us. I cannot imagine a Christian taking what appears to be a flippant attitude toward Christ any more than most Buddhists would. And yet, Christians can be reminded that simply invoking the name of Jesus or mindlessly conforming to external authority of church or tradition is not the same thing as responding to the reality conveyed through Christ. Moreover, Christians can also be challenged to be thinking people, not to accept truth claims mindlessly. I will say more about this later in this book, but here I note again that we have something to learn from the way thoughtful Buddhists respond to Buddha and later Buddhist leaders.

What about Buddhist scriptures? To what extent are they authoritative? The Dhammapada, remembered sayings of the Buddha, is primary. I have relied mainly on the Dhammapada in this chapter, considering its sayings to be the most important source of Buddhist teaching. This work was not written by the Buddha himself. Indeed, he may not have written anything; in any event, no writing by the Buddha was passed on. Nor, for that matter, was the Dhammapada written in the Buddha's own language. (Christian scholars would find this problem familiar, since the earliest versions of the New Testament were written in Greek, not in Jesus' own Aramaic language.) After the Buddha's death, around 483 BCE, the monks closely associated with him sought to preserve his teachings. A council was held, memories shared, the Buddha's personal attendant Ananda delegated to organize his recollections of the Buddha's principal teachings. The resultant body of teachings was passed on orally for generations before being committed to writing around the third century BCE. Different versions have existed, but the main body of teaching has been accepted in various Buddhist traditions. Can non-Buddhists accept this as authentic expressions of the Buddha himself? With due allowances for some variations, we can note that oral transmission of even larger bodies of tradition can be surprisingly accurate. In any event, the process is not limited to Buddhism.

So the text of the Dhammapada is revered by Buddhists. But that does not mean that Buddhists of the various schools treat these sayings legalistically. They can be regarded as pointers to the truth, not as words that in and of themselves bring human fulfillment. The Dhammapada makes that very clear. We read:

If one, though reciting much of texts
Is not a doer thereof, a heedless man;
He, like a cowherd counting others' cows,
Is not a partaker in the religious quest.

One must embody the truth through action for its reality to be effective. Even those who are not acquainted with the teachings can be drawn into the reality by the way they live.

> If one, though reciting little of texts,
> Lives a life in accord with dhamma (truth),
> Having discarded passion, ill will, and unawareness,
> Knowing full well, the mind well freed,
> He is not grasping here, neither hereafter,
> Is a partaker of the religious quest.

Of course, that is already basic Christian teaching: "For it is not the hearers of the law who are righteous in God's sight, but the doers of the law who will be justified" (Rom. 2:13) and "But be doers of the word, and not merely hearers who deceive themselves" (Jas. 1:22). So, in addition to finding reinforcement in the Buddhist teaching, Christians can be warned of the perils of the kind of religious fundamentalism that places undue emphasis on mechanical acceptance of the Bible as an end in itself. Scripture points toward the deeper reality; it is not itself the supreme authority.

The Illusion of Permanence

We come to a central tenet of virtually all forms of Buddhism: the things we cherish in this life are mostly illusion, and many Buddhists would substitute "all" for "mostly" in that sentence. Everything has a short shelf life. One is reminded of the old German folk song: "All things shall perish from under the sky, music alone shall live, never to die." Except that Buddhists would not exempt music from the universal fate of all phenomena! They might prefer the lines from the book of Ecclesiastes in the Hebrew Bible we have already cited: "Vanity of vanities, says the Teacher. . . . All is vanity. . . . All things are wearisome; more than one can express" (Eccl. 1:2, 8). Nothing, in the end, brings fulfillment. Not transitory moments of happiness, not the accumulation of wealth and property, not power, nor prestige; not a record of accomplishments suitable for a resume. Not even life itself, for we have our physical bodies, as it were, only on loan. In this respect, Buddhism has much in common with Hinduism.

Christians may consider preoccupation with the illusions of life to be too pessimistic, but isn't there a whole lot of truth in this? We may spend a lifetime pursuing wealth, but to what end? Consider: A billionaire dies. Here was a person who had wealth far beyond the imagining of most of us. Think of the luxuries that would buy: mansions, yachts, the private jet, servants at beck and call, the ability to travel anywhere, at any time, absolutely first class. And think of the *power* that would confer, if we are interested in that, the ability to buy politicians (by purely legal means, of course). And absolutely first-rate medical care. All of that. And *still*, the billionaire has died! It hardly seems fair! We may think of such wealth as permanent, but of course it is not.

Isn't that also true of long-term name recognition? Much of my life has been devoted to academic pursuits, serving on college and seminary faculties, teaching, writing books, and so forth. Being honest with myself, while also observing colleagues through the years, I know what a premium we place on recognition of our work: to see our work in print, preferably well reviewed; to be recognized by scholarly societies; to be named to a prestigious professorship at a prestigious institution. Yes! But how long will the glow last? It can be instructive to inspect the once-prominent books in any library a few decades after their peak, when their authors are scarcely remembered, if at all. Even the books themselves will ultimately crumble into dust, no matter what kind of paper they are printed on or however they may be digitally preserved. It is an illusion to think that our words or our name will be long remembered.

Then suppose you get to be president of the United States. Your name will be remembered much longer than most of us, perhaps even a thousand years. But ten thousand years? A million years? A billion years? One way or another the universe will be around a billion years from now. Current estimates are that the universe is now about 13.7 billion years old. In due course, though nobody knows exactly how, the universe will cease to be. The earth may last a few billion years more if we don't blow it up. But humanity? In the evolutionary course of things, human beings came into being perhaps two or three million years ago. And recorded history dates from just a few thousand years back. In cosmic terms, that is not a very long time. So how can we expect to be remembered in the long run?

The Buddhist cosmology and its account of human life, with cycles of reincarnation, is not the same as the Christian worldview. But haven't we something to learn from the Buddhist recognition that *things* don't last?

That may be an especially important lesson among Christians in the West, whose cultures place inordinate emphasis on the acquisition of things, thereby stimulating materialistic greed. The materialistic goal is illusory, says Buddhism. So also says Christianity, but the insight has often been lost in the deluge of cultural pressures. At one level, Christians may affirm their faith and seek to practice it; at another, sometimes more decisive, level, they may be driven by illusory values.

There remains a problem for both Buddhists and Christians. What Buddhists consider to be illusory and Christians can at least consider to be ephemeral does have some reality. After all, we do live in this world where we must come to terms, somehow, with our physical nature and that of the world. How do Buddhists deal with this? Buddha himself lived in this world. His trial run of complete asceticism was, as we have seen, abandoned after a few years—just as he had previously abandoned the wealth and power of a privileged crown prince. Instead, he affirmed a middle way. While he lived a couple of centuries before Aristotle, he would have affirmed something of the Greek philosopher's "golden mean," living a life in this world between excess and deficiency. So Buddha implicitly recognized a kind of relative truth to the illusory realm of phenomena. The Dalai Lama articulated this as he distinguished between "relative" and "absolute" truth. He writes, "If, according to absolute truth, things have no true existence, why do we speak of relative truth as *truth*? Because it is true for the perceiver. It is true for the mind clouded by ignorance, which believes in the reality of its perceptions." Absolute truth, on the other hand, is in the emptiness revealed through investigation of "the nature of the individual and of all phenomena. . . . This emptiness is an absolute truth that is apparent to the mind. . . . So when one has [seen] that no phenomena truly exist, one does not need to have this explained again or to repeat the investigation." The "emptiness," for Buddhism, is not a concept; it is an enlightenment attained after a very long process of "listening, reflecting, and meditating." It is a possibility for every human being, although few attain such enlightenment.

A Christian approach to what the Dalai Lama has called relative truth will be very different. But it can at least be comparable insofar as Christians recognize that the apparent permanence of most things is indeed illusory. Reflecting on the Buddhist perspective can sharpen that point for Christians. We create physical symbols of permanence, even in our religious life, only to discover that they crumble. We are reminded by Jesus not to lay up treasures on earth, "where moth and rust consume and where thieves break in and steal" (Matt. 6:19).

A vivid illustration of this occurred in the U.S. capital in the summer of 2011 when a moderate (5.8) earthquake shook the region. There were few injuries and not much physical damage, but the massive Washington National Cathedral suffered a good deal of the latter. The damage to this monument to ecclesial permanence brought to mind a conversation I had with a former dean of the cathedral during the 1970s. I remarked to him that I had heard that the cathedral had been built entirely of stone, without steel reinforcements. Dean Francis Sayre confirmed this, noting that steel hasn't been around long enough for us to know how many centuries it could last—and the cathedral was built, he said, to last more than a thousand years. Perhaps it will. But the building obviously can't be there forever, and the longevity of stone construction had obviously been miscalculated. A subsequent PBS special on the building of medieval cathedrals illustrated how a French cathedral was on the point of collapse some two hundred years after its thirteenth-century construction. It was saved by the artful use of well-concealed iron bars that have, so far at least, done what they were supposed to do.

We can all think of objects built to be permanent that succumbed to the ravages of time. So far, at least, the Egyptian pyramids have remained in place, thousands of years after their construction. But if lofty mountain ranges can change after thousands or millions of years, then the pyramids certainly will not be there forever. Physical permanence is illusory. Christians can learn from Buddhism how to live in accord with that undeniable fact.

Suffering

Why does it matter to Buddhists that everything is illusion except the ultimate enlightenment in which we experience a transcendent kind of emptiness? To Buddhism this is not simply a philosophical insight. Illusion matters because it is so closely related to human suffering.

Buddha's own journey toward enlightenment and becoming a Buddha, as we have seen, was occasioned by his own encounter with human suffering. His pursuit of traditional Hindu asceticism, almost to the point of starving himself to death, did not bring enlightenment, only preoccupation with his own bodily needs. So he gave that up. In time, while seated in a deep meditative trance under a tree, he achieved full enlightenment about the human condition. When we are emptied of all human illusions, we are liberated from bondage to suffering in the endless cycles of rebirth; it no longer has a hold on us. We have entered into Nirvana, the state of pure emptiness. Interpretations of the meaning of Nirvana vary among Buddhists, but the common stereotype among non-Buddhists that this is nothingness may be wide of the mark—unless that means something like no-*thing*-ness. Buddha himself declined to offer verbal interpretations.

What, then, is the root of suffering? In the words of Buddha, as remembered by his disciples in the Dhammapada, the basic problem is craving.

> The craving of a person who lives heedlessly
> Grows like a *maluva* creeper. . . .

> Whomsoever in the world
> This childish entangled craving overcomes,
> His sorrows grow. . . .

> As long as the roots are unharmed, firm,
> A tree, though toppled, grows yet again.
> Just so, when the latent craving is not rooted out,
> This suffering arises again and again.

However, "the dissolution of craving subdues all suffering." It is, one might suppose, like a person seeking to slake intense thirst by drinking seawater, leading to more thirst, not less. Just so, increasing attachment to illusory things intensifies the suffering that leads to such attachments.

The thinking of nineteenth-century German philosopher Arthur Schopenhauer can help us see what Buddha is getting at. While he was not exactly a Buddhist himself, at this point Schopenhauer's thought is strikingly parallel. According to Schopenhauer, all of life is consumed by the relentless craving to satisfy one's needs. Need is essentially pain. Even what we experience as pleasure is only the temporary satisfaction of need. Hunger is pain. Food for the hungry may seem pleasurable, but that is only because it provides a respite from the pain of hunger. We can speak similarly of other physical needs and drives, including sex. Addictions represent compulsive patterns of relief from progressively worsening pain, often taking self-destructive forms.

Such suffering can also be psychological, spiritual, or social in form. For example, an actor, a politician, or a preacher may be seeking the affirmation of crowds of people as an antidote to the accumulated pain of a neglected childhood. The acclaim of the multitude must be repeated again and again, with greater and greater intensity. A highly successful novelist may live in fear that the next novel will be a failure, thus exposing the emptiness of the previous successes. A retired politician, now out of the limelight, may find pathetic means of restoring the lost prominence. Thus, a former U.S. secretary of state—whose diplomatic service had in fact been phenomenal—pretended against his better judgment to support the Vietnam War in order to stay in the good graces of a U.S. president, continuing to be a player in the game of national and international politics. (I have that candid assessment from another prominent elder statesman of that era who was in a position to know.)

What are Christians to make of this diagnosis of the human condition? Is it as pessimistic as it seems to be? Perhaps it is only pessimistic about the illusions, the futilities, the false values around which so much human life is centered. A Christian may find positive value in many aspects of human life. Creaturely needs and their satisfactions are not altogether experienced as suffering. And yet, isn't there something to be learned from this Buddhist teaching? Isn't it true that a whole lot of our striving after the fleeting goods of this life is but an expression of underlying pain? When we are driven, is that not an all-consuming effort to relieve deeply rooted spiritual pain? When we exhibit narcissistic tendencies, is that not an expression of deeper anxieties?

For all of us, there is sorrow and the fear of death. A woman came to the Buddha to pour out her grief about the loss of her son. How could she find consolation? The Buddha tells her to go from door to door and collect a mustard seed from every house that knows no sorrow. She would not find many seeds that way! She is reminded that sorrow is a part of the human condition, experienced by almost everybody.

Christians, as well as Buddhists, do not have to live in a perpetual state of morbidness to realize that coming to terms with spiritual pain and loss is essential to spiritual freedom and serenity. The Christian route to freedom and serenity of spirit is not the same as Buddhist meditation and the quest for that ultimate state of emptiness and enlightenment. But even the Buddhist meditational exercises have been useful for many Christians who have not felt it necessary to depart from their faith as Christians. Moreover, Christians should not overlook the sheer joyfulness of a good deal of Buddhist life and practice.

Buddhist Compassion

There is still another point where Buddhist emphasis can reinforce Christian life. The Buddhist narrative about Buddha's own arrival at enlightenment and becoming a Buddha dwells on the fact that he could, at that moment, have entered into Nirvana, essentially leaving the world and its cares behind. Instead, he was profoundly moved by the suffering of all beings, and he resolved to return to the world and to do all he could to alleviate that suffering. Even as he achieved enlightenment, he became deeply compassionate.

"Compassion" means feeling with another. It is taking the suffering of others into one's own being and devoting oneself to helping the other. In traditional Buddhism, that care is not restricted to other human beings, because all sentient beings, all beings capable of feeling, are part of the same moral universe, and all beings are a part of the perpetual cycle of reincarnation from one existence to the next. In Buddhist terms, compassionate response to the other is helping the other to find liberation from the suffering of existence by further movement toward the ultimate state of enlightenment. Buddha, through his forty years as a wandering guru, attracted disciples who, in turn, expressed this same kind of compassion for others.

A noteworthy feature of Buddhist compassion is an unwillingness to be judgmental toward others in their frailties. Buddhists have not been perfect in that regard; in common with the rest of humanity, they are subject to frailties. Still, among the great world religions, Buddhism stands out for its tolerance and caring attitude toward others. That is something that Buddhists share with Christians at their best. The Christian sense of God's grace is, in principle, accepting of all despite their imperfections. And yet, relatively speaking, Christians have also been more prone to judge and condemn. Perhaps Buddhism can inspire Christians to embrace afresh the truer, deeper implications of love.

In that respect, I am struck by the specific ethical teachings of Buddhism, often paralleling the moral wisdom in the Sermon on the Mount, the parables of Jesus, and the great thirteenth chapter of Paul's First Letter to the Corinthians. Consider this Buddhist set of beatitudes:

> When a need has arisen, friends are a blessing.
> A blessing is contentment with whatever [there be].
> A blessing is the wholesome deed at the end of life.
> A blessing it is to relinquish all sorrow.
>
> A blessing in the world is reverence for mother.
> A blessing, too, is reverence for father.
> A blessing in the world is reverence for the recluse.
> A blessing too is reverence for the *brahmana*.
>
> A blessing is virtue into old age.
> A blessing is faith established.
> A blessing is the attainment of insight-wisdom.
> A blessing it is to refrain from doing wrongs.

These teachings of Buddha are not exactly the same as the New Testament Beatitudes in Matthew 5. But similarities are not limited to the form of teaching. Most of these Buddhist ethical teachings are fully consistent with Christian insight, and some of them, such as "reverence for the recluse," are worth pondering as additions to Christian teaching. Another mark of these Buddhist teachings is their consideration of the whole span of life, such as "the wholesome deed at the end of life" and "virtue into old age."

I am struck by the apparent conflict between the Buddhist counsel to "relinquish all sorrow" and the Christian beatitude "blessed are those who mourn." There is probably some truth in both, and Christians might rightly protest that it is unhealthy to repress grief. Still, is it not also true that clinging to sorrow for the rest of one's life can be at least as unhealthy? Haven't we all known people who simply could not let go, sometimes with morbid attachment to objects associated with a deceased loved one? The Buddhist teaching about relinquishing sorrow could at least be a corrective at that point.

The apostle Paul's writing in 1 Corinthians 13 also has interesting Buddhist parallels. For instance, Paul writes that "love is patient; love is kind; love is not envious or boastful or arrogant or rude." And then we have, from Buddha, such sayings as "let one not live envying others" and "who would speak speech that is true, that is instructive and not harsh, by which one would anger none—that one I call a *brahmana*."

Love has a central place in both traditions. The Dalai Lama pointedly challenges Christians: "If, for example, a Christian truly loves God, then he should practice love for all his fellow human beings." There have always been Christians who have passed such a test; regrettably, many have not. I do not know that Buddhist teaching about the importance of love has anything in particular to add to Christian teaching at this point. But Christians can certainly gain inspiration from the example of saintly Buddhists and greater appreciation for how the moral impetus toward love is built into our created humanity.

The Law of Karma

How, then, are we to deal with what Christians call sin? Is there a Buddhist equivalent?

While emphasizing compassion for human suffering, with a generally positive attitude toward others, Buddhism has a clear, sometimes almost rigid, sense that all of our actions, good and bad, have consequences. When we do good things, we become better people. When we act against the good, we fall more deeply into the rut of the endless cycles of suffering. Eknath Easwaran, a leading interpreter of the Buddhist Dhammapada, writes of the law of Karma: "Every event, mental or physical, has to have effects, whether in the mind, in action, or in both—and each such effect becomes a cause itself." Thus, he continues, "To the Buddha, the universe is a vast sea where any stone thrown raises ripples among billions of other ripples. Karma raises ripple-effects within personality and without, for both are in the same field of forces. When we pursue our own self-interest, we are adding to a sea of selfish behavior in which we too live. Sooner or later, the consequences cannot help but come back to us." So the Buddha has put it this way: "Fly in the sky, burrow the ground, you cannot escape the consequences of your actions." Or as Easwaran adds, "You can run, but you cannot hide. All of us have karmic scores to settle, a book of debits and credits that is constantly growing." And so Buddha is led to believe in the cycle of death and rebirth.

Translated into the doctrine of reincarnation, we make our progression more difficult. Christians, again, are not likely to accept the notion of reincarnation. But the long-term effects of our actions on character formation can be equally clear. The traditional Christian contrast between virtues and vices gains new emphasis in this context. Both virtue and vice can be habit forming. In traditional language, a virtue is a habit of the will toward a good end, while a vice is a habit headed in the opposite direction. There is this difference between typical Christian and Buddhist positions: While Christians may be more inclined to blame people with deep-seated vices, Buddhists are more often compassionate in their sense of the humanity of such people, wanting to help liberate them from the illusions upon which such Karma is based.

Whether or not that is so, Christians do well to ponder, along with Buddhists, the clear fact that actions have consequences, not only in the world affected by the actions, but also in the spirit of the actor. A cutthroat businessperson who considers employees nothing but instruments to be used in the acquisition of wealth cannot escape a coarsening of spirit, the loss of human sensitivity, deep unhappiness. For good or ill, we largely become what we do. Still, both for Buddhists and for Christians, the appropriate response to what Buddhists call the law of Karma is not fatalistic surrender to forces beyond our control. Christians speak of repentance and new life; Buddhists encourage sufferers to take steps toward enlightenment.

The Lotus Sutra and Soka Gakkai

Beyond general points of agreement among Buddhists, the different versions of Buddhism offer more or less unique interpretations of the main themes. It is beyond the scope of this book to explore all of these, but I am particularly struck by the contemporary Soka Gakkai International movement (SGI) and, in particular, the emphasis it places on the Lotus Sutra as a principal Buddhist scripture.

The Lotus Sutra is one of the more challenging scriptures among the world religions, in part because of its frequent repetitions with slightly different twists and turns. The repetitiveness is not, in itself, overly burdensome, but it may make the text less gripping. The greater difficulty is distinguishing between historical fact and vast exaggerations. For instance, we frequently read there that the Buddha is surrounded by eighty thousand bodhisattvas (enlightened followers headed toward Buddhahood) who are there to pose questions. That's enough people to fill a large football stadium! In another place, the Buddha is approached by eight hundred billion bodhisattvas. That is more than a hundred times the world's present population. And to indicate the vastness of time in the past when a Buddha lived, we read that "if a person should use his strength to smash the ground of the major world system, should completely crush its earth particles and reduce them all to powdered ink, and if he continued in this manner until he had exhausted all the specks of ink, and if one then took the soil of the lands he had passed through, both those he dropped a speck in and those he did not, and once more ground their earth into dust, and then took one grain of dust to represent one *kalpa*—the number of tiny grains of dust in the past would be less than the number of *kalpas* in the past when that Buddha lived." With one *kalpa* defined as an exceedingly long period of time, the result of the calculation could be a longer time span than the age of the universe. So here we have a very colorful way to characterize time.

These and other exaggerations are, in context, employed to emphasize large numbers of people or lengths of time, perhaps not unlike Jesus' admonition that we should remove the log in our own eye before attempting to remove the speck in somebody else's. What are we to make of it? In part, the Sutra explains itself by frequently asserting that it is necessary for the Buddha to use "expedient means" to draw people into confrontation with the central teaching of the truth, which otherwise they would not see. That means that we should say what will be most useful, not necessarily what is literally true. As an illustration of this, the Buddha offers a parable about a rich man whose children are playing games in his great mansion that has caught fire. They will not be distracted from their games without the promise of a gift, available only if they will leave the house. The gift is illusory, but the children do leave the burning house. The rich man then gives them something more valuable than what had been promised. Was this a lie? Perhaps in one sense. But it was necessary to save their lives and to provide an even greater treasure. Thus, people are approached on a level they can understand in order to be drawn into the deeper meaning. So if by expedient means we help people come to true enlightenment, we have, by that means, provided them with the most profound treasure.

That teaching of the Lotus Sutra might remind Christians that it is sometimes necessary to use stories or parables that are not literally true to draw others into greater truth. Do we here have a Buddhist justification for the use of myth, even when a myth is temporarily treated as factual? It is at least a reminder that people are at different stages in their spiritual development. We should never assume that we are all at the same stage. A child may find Santa Claus to be a kindly giver of gifts, an expression of love, even though adults know perfectly well that Santa Claus does not exist. Parents may still encourage that belief, seating the child on a department store Santa's lap, listening carefully to what the child says that she or he wants for Christmas, and doing their Christmas shopping accordingly. Only later can the child perceive that those gifts express the factual love of parents and others and that the parental love is much more important than Santa Claus.

The Lotus Sutra refers to those who reject its central teaching as thereby destined to endless reincarnations of suffering. Still, it often pictures the possibility that everyone might become a Buddha. One of the necessary conditions of becoming a Buddha is that one should selflessly express compassion for all, even when rejected and persecuted. Nobody is to be treated as an enemy. That is not unlike the Christian emphasis on loving one's enemies.

References in the Lotus Sutra to the "law" can be misleading if the word is taken in its usual sense. The Sutra does not mean law in any legislated or legalistic sense; it is not an external rule to regulate conduct. It refers to the doctrine that the Buddha is teaching, the dharma. There is even a sense that this is a pervasive reality, infused throughout all being. The Soka Gakkai movement sees this reality as present to all of us, waiting to be unlocked. As Daisaku Ikeda, SGI president, put it in his foreword to a Lotus Sutra edition:

> The Lotus Sutra clearly and definitively reveals the buddha nature that is an integral part of the lives of all people. And it makes clear that the Buddha desires and acts so that all people, by opening up this buddha nature inherent within themselves, may attain the state of buddhahood for themselves. . . . The buddha nature, which is inherent in all living beings, is a universal and fundamental source or fountain of hope. When it is fully brought to light, it allows all human beings to realize their highest level of personal development and to attain unparalleled happiness and good fortune. And the Lotus Sutra is the text that most forcefully asserts this truth.

For us, this statement has three implications. First, it may lead us to rethink the typical Christian characterization of Buddhism as atheistic. True, the dharma of Buddhism is not the same as the Christian God. But it is a positive, living, and eternal reality of which we are invited to partake. This is a far cry from viewing reality as empty. To be sure, Buddhism does regard attachments to the passing phenomena of life as illusion. But we are still invited to relate to human existence wisely and in the context of the eternal dharma. This is pictured in the Lotus Sutra as rich and joyful, fully positive. As another Soka Gakkai leader has put it, things still have meaning. There is wisdom here about how to navigate in life, how to live a better life.

A second implication of the Ikeda quotation is that all of life, in fact everything in the universe, is deeply interconnected. Nothing has completely independent existence. Nothing arises independently. While it is an illusion to think of any existing thing as permanent, it is equally an illusion to see anything as coming into being all by itself. That, too, is an insight that Christians can embrace. One of the reasons that some Christians resist the scientific theory of evolution is that it seems to deny the work of a divine creator. However, Christians who accept evolution consider this a factual explanation of how creation developed. Maybe the story of the creation of Adam and Eve in the garden of Eden is mythological, but that does not mean that God did not create the forces that could proceed in the long course of evolution. By any account, nothing has happened that was not potential from the beginning. Both Buddhist and Christian scriptural accounts of the origins of life can be misleading if taken in literal detail. But both can underscore the mystery of origins and the profound interconnectedness of all being.

So another implication of this view of Buddhism is that there are spiritual disciplines that can lead to our awakening to this dimension of life. It is already present within us, waiting to be unlocked. Buddhist disciplines emphasize contemplation, sustained periods of meditation.

Can Christians learn from this? Perhaps not, if we think of meditation as an end in itself and if this requires particular forms of meditation. But if it is meditation in the expectation of enlightenment, and if enlightenment is not divorced from human responsibility in the world, then the Buddhist teaching may not be that far removed from the insights of a good deal of Christian mystic literature.

Is there a Buddhist understanding of the nature of human responsibility that can enrich Christians? I am struck by the repeated emphasis on compassion. Spiritual disciplines are of no use when they do not lead to greater love. The point is registered in a good deal of Buddhist literature. One striking illustration in the Lotus Sutra appears in a discussion of how people can discipline the evils related to six sense organs (eye, ear, mind, nose, tongue, body). Taking up evil speaking of the tongue, the Sutra holds that "if one wishes to control and tame it, one must diligently practice pity and compassion." It is not enough to control or repress evil tendencies. One must focus on the good of compassion.

In sum, the Soka Gakkai expression of Buddhism calls for what Bill Aiken, director of the SGI center in Washington, DC, refers to as a "balanced spiritual diet." The wisdom gained through enlightenment is partly about how to navigate in life, how to live a better life. It is not life denying; it is more about human fulfillment than spiritual emptiness, although one must empty oneself of illusions and false values and embrace our interconnectedness with all aspects of reality.

Questions for Discussion

1. Why do most Buddhists refuse to talk about God? Is Buddhism essentially atheistic?
2. What can we learn from the Buddhist view that life is filled with illusions? Are there aspects of our lives that are built on illusions?
3. Are Christian views of the suffering Christ compatible with the Buddhist view of the enlightened and unflappable Buddha?
4. Is the Buddhist commitment to compassion similar to Christian love?
5. Can someone be a Christian and a Buddhist at the same time?

Chapter 7

Learning from Chinese Religion

The universe is everlasting.
The reason the universe is everlasting
Is that it does not live for Self.
Therefore it can long endure.
Therefore the Sage puts himself last,
And finds himself in the foremost place.

—Lao-tzu

As befitting its long history and immense size, China presents us with many complexities. That certainly applies to China's religious traditions. A *Washington Post* article in 2011 exploring what may be a breakdown in moral sensitivity in China quotes economics professor Hu Xingdon as saying that present-day Chinese "don't have beliefs, although China has indigenous religions like Taoism and Buddhism. . . . China is actually an atheist country, and Chinese people are never afraid of God's punishment." The Communist Party that has ruled China for more than sixty years is, of course, officially atheist. In recent years, Maoist Marxism has lost much of its appeal in China, even in ruling party circles. It is debatable to what extent atheism permeates the popular culture of this land of more than a billion people. I will deal with atheism as a religion in chapter 9.

Taoism and Confucianism are the most important traditional Chinese religions. The *Tao Te Ching* contains the wise sayings attributed to Lao-tzu. The *Analects* of Confucius are attributed to that formative Chinese thinker. These are foundational collections. While I have relied on them in this chapter, the reader should be aware that traditional Chinese religion is vast and complex, with other sources and interrelationships, including the substantial Buddhist presence. Still, Lao-tzu and Confucius are the most influential and best-known "founders."

Lao-tzu (or Laotse), the philosopher who was basically the founder of Taoism, was born around 571 BCE (although his dates continue to be debated by scholars). Confucius, originator of Confucianism, was born around 551 BCE, so the two may have been contemporaries. In some respects, Taoism and Confucianism represent contrasting tendencies in religious thought, although it may be more accurate to say that they were and are complementary. Each presents us with a bundle of aphorisms, wise sayings intended to guide people who want to be wise in their attitudes and actions. Of the two, Taoism is the more explicitly religious, constantly referencing the Eternal Tao as the source of existence and wisdom. Confucianism presents an array of sayings that are especially relevant to the conduct of leaders and the proper functioning of society. The two could coexist for many centuries as formative influences in Chinese culture. Taoism and Confucianism also coexisted with forms of Buddhism.

The wise sayings in both Taoism and Confucianism include many that reinforce insights present in Christian tradition. Still, Christians do well to ponder a number of these sayings as an enrichment of their own faith and practice. The values to be gained here are not unlike those in the book of Proverbs in Hebrew Scripture. I have selected a number of these from the basic Taoist scripture, the *Tao Te Ching,* and from the *Analects* of Confucius.

The Wisdom of Tao

A central religious insight of Tao is that the Eternal Tao cannot be named. The basis of all life and wisdom is beyond human words. The wisdom of Tao can be stated, as the *Tao Te Ching* endeavors to do. But the Tao itself is beyond comprehension. So the very first words of the remembered teachings of Lao-tzu are "Tao can be talked about, but not the Eternal Tao. Names can be named, but not the Eternal Name. As the origin of heaven and earth, it is nameless."

Of course, even the Taoist refers to the Tao! Lao-tzu struggles with the problem of how to speak of Tao without giving Tao a name:

> Before the Heaven and Earth existed
> There was something nebulous
>> Silent, isolated,
>> Standing alone, changing not,
>> Eternally revolving without fail,
>> Worthy to be the Mother of all Things.

I do not know its name
   And address it as Tao.
If forced to give it a name, I shall call it "Great."

Christians have always used names for God—"Father" being perhaps most frequently voiced in prayer. But the Taoist view that no name can be given for the "Eternal Name" is a reminder that no human name can encompass the wholeness of God. Of course the references to Tao are not fully consistent with Christian understandings of God. There is a sense, however, in which the nature of Tao is best expressed in the wisdom writings of the *Tao Te Ching*. One might similarly argue that a Christian understanding of God is best contained in the Christian teachings about the will of God—for the nature of God is revealed in the purposes of God. If that is so, a Christian might ponder the proverbs of the *Tao Te Ching* that express the nature of Tao with a sense that a number of them also tell us more about the nature of the God who is worshiped by Christians.

Consider this, for example, as a subtle view of the reality of God:

There is nothing weaker than water
But none is superior to it in overcoming the hard,
For which there is no substitute.
That weakness overcomes strength
And gentleness overcomes rigidity,
No one does not know;
No one can put into practice.

There is, here and there in the *Tao Te Ching*, an understanding of the source of human conflict. One example is this provocative passage:

Exalt not the wise,
   So that the people shall not scheme and contend;
Prize not rare objects,
   So that the people shall not steal;
Shut out from sight the things of desire,
   So that the people's hearts shall not be disturbed.

Conflict, in this saying, is grounded in competition. Eliminating competition from human society does not seem very realistic, and possibly not even desirable. Moreover, exalting the wise may be an important way to encourage people to develop wisdom themselves. Still, too easy a division between "winners" and "losers" in human society does give rise to conflict. A fair amount of Christian rhetoric is reinforced by this Taoist passage—such as Paul's characterization of the church as the "body of Christ" in which no members should think themselves superior to any other. The Taoist principle can be a word of caution to Christians who subordinate communal values and fellow feeling to competitive values.

In a similar vein, we are counseled by the *Tao* not to put ourselves before others. The Sage—that is, the wise one—"wants to remain behind [even though he] finds himself at the head of others." Then, "is it not because he is selfless that his Self is realized?" I am struck by that as it pertains to status within institutional churches. For example, leadership roles in churches should not be sought after to enhance one's status. For Christians, the story of Jesus washing his disciples' feet on that last night before the crucifixion is a reminder that we are called to serve, not to dominate. And, according to the *Tao*, when we have completed the work we have set out to do, we should get out of the way! "When you have done your work, retire."

In words that would be affirmed by environmentalists, the *Tao* states that "the world is a sacred vessel, which must not be tampered with or grabbed after. To tamper with it is to spoil it, and to grasp it is to lose it." To speak of the world as a "sacred vessel" is akin to regarding it as having its source in Tao. The same section of the *Tao* counsels moderation, however, not taking extreme positions. "The Sage," it advises, "avoids all extremes, excesses and extravagances." There is a time and a place for everything—a point emphasized in that same section in language similar to the familiar litany of Ecclesiastes 3 about there being "a time for" this and for that. Christians have not always been careful in dealing with ideological absolutes of one kind or another, by either blind acceptance of an ideology or total rejection. Most ideological options ought to be treated as relatively good or relatively unacceptable, recognizing that there are usually some redeeming factors in the latter and some flaws in the former.

The *Tao* contains warnings about war. While not exactly pacifist in tone, the writing is realistic about the dangers and evils of war. "As weapons are instruments of evil, they are not properly a gentleman's instruments; only on necessity will he resort to them. For peace and quiet are dearest to his heart, and to him even a victory is no cause for rejoicing." That last point is emphasized: "To rejoice over a victory is to rejoice over the slaughter of men! Hence a man who rejoices over the slaughter of men cannot expect to thrive in the world of men." Christians caught up in the fervor of war need to heed that word from what they are bound to consider an unlikely source. The *Tao* seems to suggest something like the traditional "just war" position, but it can help to emphasize that even when a war is considered to be justified, it is always tragic. It always involves vast suffering and sorrow. It often gives rise to war crimes, on all sides. Is it possible to engage in military conflict while fully conscious of its tragedies and while resolved to minimize the suffering? Christian pacifists doubt it. Most Christians are not pacifists, but even so they must always remember the biblical counsel to love one's enemies and to seek to be peacemakers.

The *Tao*'s counsel to rulers is in this same vein. A wise ruler "does not try to override the world with force of arms." In language reminiscent of the biblical "all who take the sword will perish by the sword" (Matt. 26:52), the *Tao* asserts that "it is in the nature of a military weapon to turn against its wielder." The effect on the community can be catastrophic: "After a great war, bad years invariably follow." Even after victory, the saying continues,

> You must not parade your success.
> You must not boast of your ability.
> You must not feel proud.
> You must rather regret that you had not been able to
> prevent the war.
> You must never think of conquering others by force.

This thought is expressed in a striking phrase that Christians might well take to heart: War, according to Tao, "is treated on a par with a funeral service. Because many people have been killed, it is only right that survivors should mourn for them. Hence, even a victory is a funeral." Reading those words sets me to thinking what it might be like for churches to hold funeral services at the conclusion of a war to mourn and honor the dead on both sides. If the outcome of a war has been to liberate a people from oppression or to thwart an unjust invasion, one can be grateful that these ends have been accomplished. Still, the war itself will have brought evil and tragedy to the lives of many people. A time of mourning over that reality can be fully consistent with affirming the justice of the cause for which the war was fought.

Rulers, according to the *Tao,* should be self-effacing, governing quietly, almost invisibly. "The highest type of ruler is one of whose existence the people are barely aware." Indeed, "when [the ruler's] task is accomplished and things have been completed, all the people say, 'We ourselves have achieved it!'" By that standard, leaders are not preoccupied by how much credit they receive nor their own legacy. Their sole concern is with the good they can accomplish, for its own sake.

The *Tao* includes a serious indictment of materialism. "An excessive love for anything will cost you dear in the end. The storing up of too much goods will entail a heavy loss. To know when you have enough is to be immune from disgrace." And "There is no calamity like not knowing what is enough. There is no evil like covetousness. Only he who knows what is enough will always have enough." And "The Sage desires to be desireless, sets no value on rare goods." And "He who knows when he has got enough is rich." Such views anticipate the later teachings of Jesus (as in, "Do not store up for yourselves treasures on earth, where moth and rust consume and where thieves break in and steal," [Matt. 6:19]). But what about the actual views and values of millions of contemporary Christians?

The *Tao* does not put much stock in ceremony, reminding us perhaps of the words of Amos 5:21, "I hate, I despise your festivals, and I take no delight in your solemn assemblies." The *Tao* remarks that "failing morality, man resorts to ceremony. Now, ceremony is the merest husk of faith and loyalty; it is the beginning of all confusion and disorder." We should prefer "what is within to what is without." What, then, of our services and liturgies, our sacramental ceremonies and observances? I doubt that many Christians would feel prompted by those words of *Tao* to give up all outward rituals and ceremonies, nor should we. Christian liturgies can be powerful moments of reconnecting with what truly matters in life, including the claims of social justice. But when ceremonies of any kind become ends in themselves, substituting form for the deeper realities of faith and life, then the point of the *Tao* is a call to those deeper realities. I am particularly struck by how a kind of liturgical fundamentalism—treating particular forms as necessary and using them as a means of exclusion—can invade churches. If I had excluded the Buddhists from the Communion service to which I referred in chapter 6, might I not have lost something that the *Tao* has reminded us of in its comments about ceremonies?

Less controversial are the *Tao's* words extolling kindness. "The Sage has no interests of his own, but takes the interests of the people as his own. He is kind to the kind; he is also kind to the unkind; for virtue is kind." And "Requite injury with kindness." One recalls the words of Paul that "love is patient" and "kind" (1 Cor. 13:4). And to be "kind to the unkind" is akin to the love of our enemies to which we are called as Christians. What difficult words! How complex the problems we face in translating them into actions that are truly helpful. And yet, the attitude toward which we are directed, by both the gospel and the *Tao*, can be as simple as it is difficult. The *Tao* enjoins us to a life of virtue at all levels—in our own person, in our families, in the community, in the state, in the world—a reminder that there should be no separation between a personal and a social ethic.

The Sayings of Confucius

Should Confucianism be classified as a religion? That question has been much debated, because many of the remembered sayings of "the master" pertain to personal behavior and social norms rather than transcendent realities. In a careful examination of this question, Huston Smith writes, "If religion is taken in its widest sense, as a way of life woven around a people's ultimate concerns, Confucianism clearly qualifies." We are, furthermore, struck by the frequency with which Confucius refers to the way of heaven or the authority of heaven. What is heaven? Confucius evidently shared the view of heaven as the company of ancestors, led by the supreme ancestor Shang Ti. It is clear that Confucius gave high status to the wisdom of past generations in his understanding of how present life should be organized and conducted. His remembered words: "I was not born to wisdom: I loved the past, and sought it earnestly there" (Book 7.19).

What are Christians to learn from this? It reinforces the Christian view that we must not be self-centered. For instance, in response to a disciple's question, "Is there one word by which we may walk till life ends?" Confucius replied, "Fellow-feeling, perhaps. Do not do unto others what thou would not have done to thee" (15.23). This version of what Christians know as the Golden Rule appears also in his statement of the meaning of love: "to treat the people as though we tendered the great sacrifice; not to do unto others what we would not they should do unto us" (12.2).

But that is not all. Confucius's sayings about love blend easily with his emphasis on courtesy. Christians who may be prone to reduce the meaning of love to subjective feelings can find here a helpful emphasis on the disciplines of love. Feelings are important. But a rounded understanding of love includes commitments and behaviors that go beyond feelings. Confucius lived centuries before the apostle Paul, but he would have resonated with Paul's description of love in 1 Corinthians 13: "Love is patient; love is kind; love is not jealous or boastful or arrogant or rude." Those attributes of love are anticipated in much of Confucius's emphasis on courtesy. We are, he said, to behave like gentlemen, taking that term to include persons of both genders. We are to be kind to others; we are to defer to others; we are not to humiliate others. So he could say, "Love is to conquer self and turn to courtesy. If we could conquer self for one day, all below heaven would turn to love. . . . [Love is] to be always courteous of ear; to be always courteous in word and courteous in deed. . . . Love is slow to speak" (12.1, 3).

Courtesy does not simply refer to an Emily Post–style etiquette, although that might be a part of it. One way to describe it is to say that courtesy means having respect for others. To respect other persons is to have due regard for their personhood. It is possible to disagree, even to argue, with others. We can be firm in our convictions, resolute in our purposes, persuaded of the rightness of our beliefs. But even in disagreement over an issue, courtesy is to consider that this is a real person we are disagreeing with. It is, perhaps, also to take our own fallibility into account. We could be wrong; the other person might be right. Confucius, by tradition the wisest of the wise, could even be remembered as disavowing the extent of his own wisdom (9.7). A gentleman, he says, is one who speaks with humility. That brings to mind a television debate I had some years ago with the Rev. Jerry Falwell. He and I were on opposite sides of almost every question. But during a break, we conversed about our grandchildren, which, for us, was common ground. That didn't diminish the weight of the issues we had been debating, but I think it was a needed reminder of our common humanity and, perhaps, an invitation toward greater humility and civility in the way we conducted such debates.

In a version of what, in our time, has come to be referred to as tough love, Confucius asks, "Can he love thee that never tasks thee? Can he be faithful that never chides?" (14.8). Still, one should focus first on one's own flaws: "By asking much of self and little of other men ill feeling is banished." And "A high will, or a loving heart, will not seek life at cost of love. To fulfill love they will kill the body"(15.8). And "Right is the stuff of which a gentleman is made. Done with courtesy, spoken with humility, rounded with truth, right makes a gentleman. . . . His shortcomings trouble a gentleman; to be unknown does not trouble him. . . . A gentleman is firm, not quarrelsome; a friend, not a partisan" (15.17–20).

A fascinating portrait of Confucius's own courteous demeanor is contained in book 10 of the *Sayings of Confucius*. Here are parts of that portrait:

> Among his own country folk Confucius wore a homely look, like one that has no word to say.
> In the ancestral temple and at court his speech was full, but cautious.
>
> On coming back from court after his stables had been burnt, the Master said, Is anyone hurt? He did not ask about the horses.
>
> On going into the Great Temple he asked about everything.
>
> When a friend died, who had no home to go to, he said, It is for me to bury him.

Even if he knew him well, his face changed when he saw a mourner. Even when he was in undress, if he saw anyone in full dress, or a blind man, he looked grave.

Such evidences of personal courtesy might suggest that Confucius's ethical views were highly individualistic. That would miss the point. To Confucius no clear line of demarcation could be drawn between personal courtesy and public responsibility. Indeed, his concern for courteous behavior was directly related to the broader social sphere. Confucius lived during a tumultuous era of Chinese history, a time of murderous conflict and struggle between warring kingdoms and competing aspirants for royal status. His call for personal courtesy was, at the same time, a plea for greater civility in public life. Contemporary Christians can draw an important lesson from the example of Confucius: the development of traditions of mutual respect, courtesy, and civility can be important in moderating the conflicts of our time. That has to do not only with Christian attitudes and behaviors toward non-Christians and the perceived enemies of the nations in which Christians find themselves. It also can say something to us about our attitudes and behaviors toward other Christians with whom we are in conflict, as I was with the late Jerry Falwell.

Confucius also has much to say about wise governance. When he was asked to speak of kingcraft, he replied that a ruler must be concerned about three things: "food enough, troops enough, and the trust of the people." If one of the three had to be eliminated, it should be the troops. If another, then food. For trust is most important of all: "From of old all men die, but without trust a people cannot stand" (12.7). Moreover, the rule of good people will ultimately mean that "cruelty would be conquered and putting to death done away with." But, "even if a king were to govern, a lifetime would pass before love dawned" (13.11–12). So primary reliance on force is not wise. In that respect, Confucius's view of rule is quite opposed to the much-later advice of Machiavelli—who argued that it is better for the prince to be feared than to be loved, if one must choose between the two. We remember that Machiavelli's advice to the prince was offered in a predominantly Christian setting.

Confucius was himself in and out of government, in and out of favor with rulers, and often sought out as a counselor. So some of his sayings focus on commonsense advice. For example, "Be not eager for haste; look not for small gains. Nothing done in haste is thorough, and looking for small gains big things are left undone" (13.17). In his concept of social unity, Confucius makes the point that "gentlemen unite, but are not the same. Small men are all the same, but each for himself" (13.23). Real unity requires persons of integrity but not uniformity. Such points, and many more, can enrich a Christian's approach to society.

Conclusion

These two ancient Chinese thinkers cannot be followed slavishly by Christians, nor does either fundamentally oppose basic Christian beliefs. Their sayings are often worth pondering as Christians seek wisdom in the conduct of personal life and in their approach to statecraft and, in a democratic society, their exercise of responsible citizenship.

Questions for Discussion

1. How can we use human names when we refer to God while preserving a sense that God is always greater than those names?
2. Is competitiveness the essential basis of a dynamic society? How is it possible to avoid dividing humanity into winners and losers, thus leading to conflict?
3. If, with Taoism, we understand that war is always tragic, could we grieve the suffering and death of even our bitterest enemies?
4. Is it possible to govern a society without relying primarily on force?
5. Would a congress or parliament be improved by embracing Confucius's views of courtesy and civility?

Chapter 8

Learning from Smaller Groups with Special Memories

What a strange fellowship this is, the God-seekers in every land, lifting their voices in the most disparate ways imaginable to the God of all life. How does it sound from above? Like bedlam, or do the strains blend in strange, ethereal harmony?

—Huston Smith

*C*hristianity and the religions we have considered thus far—primal religions, Judaism, Islam, Hinduism, Buddhism, and the historic Chinese faiths—are often regarded as the world's major faith traditions. What constitutes "major"? With the exception of Judaism, each of these religions has far more adherents than the other religions do, with numbers ranging from hundreds of millions to billions. Judaism can also be classified as major because of its formative influence on the two largest religions, Christianity and Islam. Should we overlook all other faiths? Can Christians learn anything from traditions other than the ones we have already considered? A small book does not have space to consider every contemporary religious phenomenon. But in this chapter, I treat four other religions briefly.

Learning from the Jains

In its beginnings, and for more than a thousand years, the Jain religion was large and influential, although today it is relatively small, with around 10 million adherents worldwide. It is one of the oldest faiths on earth. Some Jains believe their religion antedated and was an important source of Hinduism. In the contemporary world, it is not unusual for Hindus and Jains to occupy common temples and, in other ways, to practice their faiths together. The linkage between Hindus and Jains suggests that, at least ultimately, Jains have much in common with Buddhism as well, beyond the fact that Jainism, along with Hinduism and Buddhism, has its source in India. Like Buddhists and Hindus, Jains believe in reincarnation.

In common with Buddhism, Jains do not believe in a God who created the universe. To Jains, the universe has always existed and will continue forever. Factually, of course, there are problems with this belief. A good deal of scientific evidence indicates that the known universe has not always existed and that at some point it may well cease to exist, at least in its present form. The Jains could argue, however, that reality, in some form, has always been and always will be. That seems to be indisputable.

Can Christians learn something from Jainism? The Jain religion is relatively unknown among Christians, at least outside India. Some aspects of Jainism may not seem very promising, such as what many Christians would consider excessive asceticism among some Jains. More important, from our point of view, is the nearly absolute commitment of Jains to nonviolence, which they carry to great lengths. For instance, some Jains will sweep the way ahead of them as they walk to be sure they won't step on any insects. Many Jains will not eat root vegetables, such as carrots and turnips, lest they destroy the plant above ground. They are emphatically vegetarians, though not vegans—they do not consider eggs or milk to be a threat to the lives of cows or hens. Can Christians learn from this nonviolent, vegetarian tradition? Mohandas Gandhi is reputed to have been greatly influenced by Jains in his own commitment to nonviolence. If so, Christian commitments to nonviolence already owe something to Jainism via Gandhi.

Reinhold Niebuhr, who abandoned pacifism at the onset of World War II, wrote that he was glad there are Christian pacifists, because they remind us that war is horrible and that all Christians should be committed to peace as a norm. Christians must never regard violence in itself as a good thing. Even the Christian "just war" tradition considers war to be bad, to be avoided almost at all cost. It can be approved by Christians only to avoid evils that are greater than war; war has to bear the burden of proof, tested by whether it can be justified by the seven time-honored criteria. That is not the Jain position, because Jains oppose acts of violence under any circumstances. But the Jain position on violence and war can at least reinforce the Christian recognition that these evils are to be avoided if at all possible. And those Christians who commit themselves to pacifism should be honored and not ridiculed for their view.

What about vegetarianism? Again, there are Christians who have adopted that diet for moral reasons and not simply for considerations of health. Setting the disputed health questions aside, the moral case for vegetarianism can at least lead us to mitigate the cruelties inflicted on so many animals and fowls that are sources of meat. For example, consider chickens crowded together in cages for life, fattened up for the kill. Or cattle herded together in large pens with nothing to do but put on weight. At least the cattle in western range lands had a life before being shipped off for slaughter in the Chicago meatpacking industry. Perhaps we might gain something of respect for the lives of such animals, even if we do not reject eating meat. The tradition among some primal peoples of conducting little rituals of thanks to the animals killed in the hunt might preserve some of that respect.

The Jains also exhibit an openness toward other religions from which many Christians can learn. Jains are often found in interfaith contexts, including organizations and dialogues designed to promote unity and clarity about differences among the world's religions.

The Jain philosophy has been described as nonabsolutism, which does not mean the absence of a distinct worldview, with attendant convictions and a lengthy catalog of moral injunctions and religious practices. The Jain nonabsolutism is consistent with a worldview that the universe has neither beginning nor ending but is constantly changing, that all human beings have a spiritual core, and that there are real differences among human beings. Like Hindus and Buddhists, Jains emphasize the importance of Karma, with its consequences for good or ill in subsequent lives. But Jains do not find a basis here for condemning other religions, the adherents of which may also exhibit the positive characteristics of Jainism. Jains emphasize certain attitudinal values, such as:

Peace, love and friendship to all
Appreciation, respect, and delight for the achievements of others
Compassion to souls who are suffering
Equanimity and tolerance in dealing with another's thoughts, words, and actions

Jains are also urged to conform to five major vows, three restraints, and five points of carefulness. The vows are:

Nonviolence in thought, word, and deed so as not to harm any living beings
Truthfulness—speaking the harmless truth
Not stealing
Chastity—absolute purity of mind and body without sensual indulgence
Nonpossession—no attachment to things or persons

The three restraints are control of the mind, control of speech, and control of body.

The five points of carefulness are while walking, while communicating, while eating, while disposing of bodily waste, and while handling fly whisks, water gourds, and so forth (to avoid killing innocent life).

These behaviors are time-honored ways of implementing fundamental Jain principles. Some of these (such as the attitudinal values) are consistent with Christian values and can be appreciated by Christians. Clearly they reinforce the nonjudgmental side of Christian teaching. We can, perhaps, also learn something from the Jains' ability to hold nonjudgmental attitudes toward others alongside their own uncompromising disciplines. That may not be surprising, since the disciplines have to do with caring for all living things. Such caring logically includes a loving attitude toward people who do not share the basic Jain attitudes and disciplines. While the logic of that attitude would seem to apply equally to Christians as they relate to those considered to be heretics or pagans, Christian history has so often demonstrated the condemnation of those considered to be outside the pale, even to the point of brutal persecution. So the example of Jains may at least be a reminder to Christians that their most basic teachings are about love and that Christians, as well as Jains, should not condemn others.

A contemporary interpretation of Jainism puts this quite directly:

> A Jain does not attempt to convert followers of other religions and there is no social ostracism of Jains who convert to other religions. Jains in general oppose any form of proselytisation, particularly the activities of Christian missionaries, because they see it as subtly aggressive, taking undue advantage of economic deprivation and lack of education. Further, there is a strong suspicion at claims of exclusivity or uniqueness by any religious group.

Could Christians go this far? Certainly the subtle aggressiveness referred to here is hardly consistent with basic Christian values. Nor should Christians ostracize those who convert to non-Christian faiths. But what about not attempting to convert others? Christians could not accept that if it means not attempting to convince others of the love of God as revealed through Jesus Christ and the need to embrace that love as the basic meaning of life. Often, however, conversion takes on a primarily institutional accent; that is, inducing people to become members of Christian churches. It may be difficult to draw a line between inviting others to share in a community of faith and pushing people to become a part of an institution. Perhaps Christians can learn to be less oriented toward statistics!

Jainism has endured for millennia as a remarkably austere faith tradition. Not surprisingly, its austerities have not proved attractive to large numbers of people. That is also true of Christian movements marked by similar austerity. Preoccupation with spiritual disciplines can, of course, get in the way of spiritual maturity. But, when viewed as means to the greater end, a disciplined spiritual life contributes to such maturity. Many Jains have certainly illustrated that. So, without copying the specific Jain forms of discipline, Christians can learn something from them.

Learning from the Sikhs

Clad in white and gold splendor, accompanied by rhythmic drums, a choral group of Sikhs sang beautifully for hundreds of people gathered at the Washington National Cathedral for the annual InterFaith Concert in 2011. The words of their hymn, "Kahe kahe re ban khojan jayee," express the heart of the faith of this 500-year-old religion. In the English translation offered to the audience, this is the hymn:

> Why go out to search for your God in the Woods? For, though ever detached, He abides within us all: Yes, He also lives within you: As the Fragrance abides in the flower, and the reflection in the mirror, so also your God. So search Him not without, but within your heart. Know the one Lord alone, within and without. This is the Wisdom imparted by the Guru. Says Nanak, "Without Knowing oneself, One is rid not of the moss of Doubt."

This affirmation of God's presence within each of us can also resonate among Christians. But Christian rhetoric often seems to imply a more distant, though loving, God. God is depicted as the One who is "up there," or whose presence we will enter after death, as though we haven't been in God's presence all along. Prayer, on the other hand, implies that we are able to communicate directly and immediately with God, and that God can communicate with us. We may not hear, but that's our fault, not God's. The Sikh hymn speaks of God's intimate presence, employing beautiful metaphors. Knowledge of God accompanies knowing oneself, for we are most authentic as we realize ourselves with God.

Sikh scriptures emphasize the reality of God. Here are a few representative quotations from the *Japji Sahib,* bearing in mind that this is but a small sampling of the extensive scriptures.

> There is One God
> He is the supreme truth.
> He, The Creator,
> Is without fear and without hate.

> He, The Omnipresent,
> Pervades the universe.
> He is not born
> Nor does He die to be born again.
> By His grace shalt thou worship Him.
> Before time itself
> There was truth.
> When time began to run its course
> He was the truth.
> Even now, He is the truth
> And
> Evermore shall truth prevail. (Nanak)

We get the picture, from this sampling. Sikhism can be described as God-intoxicated. God is everything, and God is beyond the limits of human comprehension.

This has some similarity to the Hindu Brahman and to Jewish, Christian, and Islamic understandings of God. We find our being in and through God. Apart from God there could be no human existence, and human destiny is absolutely caught up in the reality of God. That may be even more clearly expressed in Sikh religion than in Hinduism. But the Sikh focus on God is far from the Buddhist view of reality—or the Jains' more explicit denial of God.

Like Hindus and Buddhists, Sikhs affirm the contributions of other religions. That is evident in their wholehearted participation in interfaith events (such as the InterFaith concert in Washington, DC, to which I have referred). But the Sikh religion carries this a step further. Sikh scripture *includes* the sacred writings of other faiths. The most important Sikh scripture, the lengthy (1,430-page) Guru Granth Sahib, is treated by Sikhs as a living guru or teacher. It contains the words of the founders of the Sikh religion and also "the words of various other Saints from other religions including Hinduism and Islam."

It is, of course, a bit late for Christians to consider incorporating the words of holy figures of other religions (apart from the scriptures shared with Judaism) in the Christian Bible! But, cannot such writings gain higher status among Christians? Might some of these contribute to the richness of Christian spiritual life, even in services of worship? Lest we consider this too shocking, we might remember that hymns already used in worship come from a wide variety of Christian, Jewish, and secular sources, with some marginal uses of primal religious traditions. But it is comparatively rare for Hindu, Buddhist, or Muslim figures or writings to be used in Christian worship.

The Sikh conception of life after death is similar to Hindu and Buddhist beliefs in reincarnation. As one Sikh commentator puts it, "Those who are away from God will come in the cycle of life again." But liberation from this cycle of constant rebirths comes to those who "have realized the divine spark within." For them, the "soul will merge with *Wahe Guru* (wonderful God) like a drop of ocean merges in the ocean." Most Christians would not be greatly comforted by that conception of life after death. It does remind us, however, that when we are alienated from God we have lost our bearings as human beings—and that, whatever our conception of life after death, it includes union with God. Most Christians would balk at the implication that our identity as persons is lost, and most Christians do not find the doctrine of reincarnation attractive. Still, as with Hinduism and Buddhism, the Sikh beliefs encourage us to think more deeply about those aspects of earthly existence that are time bound and therefore perishable, as we contemplate eternity with God. A lot of what we value, much of what we enjoy, would not be valued or enjoyed for all eternity.

The openness to other faith traditions is a part of the Sikh rejection of human sociological divisions. There is no room here for a caste system. As Guru Amar Das writes, "All are created from the seed of God. There is the same clay in the whole world, the potter (God) makes many kinds of pots." In the words of Guru Nanak, "Recognize the light (of God) and do not ask for the caste. There is no caste in the next world." Guru Nanak, the founder of Sikhism five hundred years ago, accepts the equality of women as he rejects social distinctions: "We are born of women, we are conceived in the womb of woman, we are engaged and married to women. We make friendship with women and the lineage continued because of woman." Nanak insisted at the beginning that women should be accepted as full participants in worship and in the community—and even on the battlefield. The ancient practice of *suti*, which required a recently widowed woman to thrust herself on her husband's funeral pyre, was explicitly rejected by Sikhs. Christians in India generally sought to end that practice, too, as has the Indian government.

Christian subordination of women has been a problem from the beginning throughout the world. That is true despite the veneration of female saints, the adoration of Mary, the idealization of motherhood, and the heroism of some female martyrs. Even now, a large majority of Christians belong to denominations that exclude women from ministry or priesthood—including the Roman Catholic Church, Eastern Orthodoxy, and a number of the Protestant evangelical denominations. The denial of a clerical or sacramental role parallels the even more emphatic exclusion of women from higher-level leadership. Major changes have occurred in the past two hundred years in mainline Protestant denominations. Illustrating this, the United Methodist General Conference of 1988 celebrated the election of the first woman to that group a hundred years earlier, though she was excluded from actual participation in that 1888 meeting. As a singular mark of progress, a female bishop presided over the 1988 celebration! But in chronological terms, Sikhs were well ahead of the Methodists. The Sikh affirmation of full equality for women antedates that of even the more progressive Christian denominations. Perhaps all Christians can gain some inspiration from Sikh values and practices at this point, thus hastening the full equality of women in all branches of Christianity.

The elaborate moral codes and practices of Sikhs may not be appealing to Christians at every point, but Christians can welcome and learn from the Sikh examples of caring for those in need and joining in the quest for social justice.

Learning from Zoroastrianism

Zoroastrianism had its origins in ancient Persia, where its dualism of light and darkness helped define its major themes. Many may assume, as I once did, that Zoroastrianism had become a dead religion. Not so. My own acquaintance with the continued vitality of this ancient faith came when I joined the board of the InterFaith Conference of Metropolitan Washington, on which that faith community was well represented. It is not a large religion, numbering some 130,000 adherents worldwide, but its presence in America—far from its original base in what is now Iran—illustrates its present international reach. While the Zoroastrian community in the Washington area is not large—several hundred at present—I have experienced it as vibrant. My wife and I had the privilege of representing the InterFaith Conference at a Zoroastrian celebration. It was beautiful, joyous, energetic, with especially colorful dancing. It was an excellent introduction to one of the main Zoroastrian themes: life is created to be joyful. That is also a Christian theme, but haven't we all known Christians for whom the faith is an unhappy, moralistic burden?

Zoroastrian dualism is much debated, and a careful definition of its meaning is not important for our purposes. Traditionally it has presented a cosmic struggle between good (Ahura Mazda) and evil (Angra Mainyu). Human beings have been created with freedom of the will. If we choose the path of righteousness, our lives will lead to peace and happiness. Otherwise, we may spend time in hell. Zoroastrianism might have influenced Christian conceptions of hell, along with its other influences on the Abrahamic religious traditions. But in Zoroastrianism the suffering of hell is not for all eternity.

The dualism does not contemplate the ultimate victory of forces of evil and darkness. In its original form, Zoroastrian dualism has little to offer Christian thought. However, we can pause to note that this religion does take evil seriously, and it does not picture evil as only mistaken views of the good. It is given to human beings to choose.

In some respects the most important choice, and the one that is most emphasized by Zoroastrians, is the uncompromising commitment to truth. We are *always* bound to be truthful! There is never an adequate reason to lie, or even to misrepresent. In this, Zoroastrianism anticipates the German philosopher Immanuel Kant, for whom truth telling was an absolute moral law. Christian ethics continues to struggle with the implications of that, because there are situations in which absolute truth telling might be irresponsible and destructive. The classic illustration is what you should do if you are a German hiding Jews and the Gestapo arrives at your door to ask whether there are any Jews about. Similarly, the pre–Civil War Underground Railway that enabled slaves to escape to freedom in the North and Canada required deception. But such extreme illustrations aside, truthfulness is essential to trust. And without trust, human relationships are fragile and Christian love is empty. Despite its inflexibility in insisting on truth telling in all situations, the Zoroastrian commitment can inspire Christians to higher standards of honesty.

Learning from Baha'i

The youngest of the religions surveyed in this book is Baha'i, founded in Iran in 1844 by the Bab, who announced the coming of Baha'u'llah. In a brief summary of the origins of Baha'i, a representative of the religion explains:

> In 1863, Bah'u'llah declared Himself as the Messenger of God foretold by the Bab and awaited by all religions. He explained that all the great Prophets of God had been sent by the same Creator for the same purpose, namely to educate humanity in accordance with its capacity to receive truth. . . . Bah'u'llah proclaimed that the primary purpose of His Revelation was to bring about the awareness of the oneness of humanity and to unify the human race. This, He said, was the next logical and inevitable stage in the maturity of human kind.

Given the lateness of its arrival, we should not be surprised that Baha'i echoes themes found in other world religions. Indeed, the Baha'i faith affirms other religions and their prophets. God's religion is one, manifested and expanded from time to time by other religions and their prophets. That development has now come to an end and, with the coming of the Bab and Baha'u'llah, humanity is invited into its fulfillment. Baha'i has emphasized the theme of unity. Humankind is one. Religion all points toward oneness, as created by God. Baha'is are respectful of other religions, even as they consider their own faith to be the full manifestation of the underlying unity of religion and humankind.

Since most of the other aspects of the Baha'i faith are anticipated by other religions, we will not pause to comment on them here. The unity theme is the Baha'i faith's signal contribution. There is a touch of irony in this: The religion most emphasizing its role as unifying the different faiths was destined to become yet another distinct religion! Nevertheless, the emphasis on unity is in itself an important contribution.

The theme of unity is not absent from Christian thought and practice, but, in contrast to the Baha'i faith, Christian churches have more typically thought of the ultimate goal of unity as drawing all others into the life of the church. It has been more difficult for Christians to see other religions as the bearers of the loving purposes of God. Sometimes Christians have thought of other religions as completely alien to those purposes, as pagans or, in extreme cases, even as enemies of God. Most Christian leaders and thinkers have not gone that far. Still, even as we learn positive things from other religions, we should not embrace syncretism—which is to treat all religions as essentially the same, reducing all to a common denominator. While we can learn from other religions, we should be critical of other faiths and of our own at points where they, and we, fall short of our deeper insights. True unity does not dilute all religion; it prizes the diversity and seeks to gain from others precisely at the point of their unique contributions.

Questions for Discussion

1. Should Christians, following the lead of Jainism, become vegetarians or even vegans?
2. Has Western society advanced as far as the Sikh ideal in respecting the full equality of women?
3. How close can we come to the Zoroastrian commitment to absolute truth telling?
4. Baha'i teaches the oneness and unity of humanity. Does religion cause more disunity than unity?

Chapter 9

Learning from Atheism

We do not rely solely upon science and reason, because these are necessary rather than sufficient factors, but we distrust anything that contradicts science or outrages reason. We may differ on many things, but what we respect is free inquiry, openmindedness, and the pursuit of ideas for their own sake.

—*Christopher Hitchens*

*I*s atheism truly to be considered a *religion*? I'm sure that very few Christians think so, and I'm confident that virtually no atheists do either! It all comes down to how you define religion. I suspect that most Christians and atheists define religion as belief in God (although we have seen that at least Buddhists and Jains do not think in those terms). If, with Paul Tillich and a number of other theologians, we define religion as our ultimate concern, then I believe that atheism qualifies. "Ultimate concern" means what concerns us most, or how we understand and relate to reality, or what is the source of our deepest values. There are different forms of atheism, of course, but most atheists conceive of reality something in the manner of Bertrand Russell's view of "omnipotent matter" rolling "on its relentless way." The universe is without ultimate purpose; it remains for humanity to construct its own purposes. Most atheists vigorously insist that their lives are governed by values, although those values are not derived in any way from a divine creator at the center of all being.

This was emphasized by a self-identified atheist, Aaron Kiely, who wrote to me, "I and many other atheists have beliefs or moral sentiments (e.g., support for the golden rule as a worthwhile principle) that collectively might somehow qualify as an 'ultimate concern.' But such beliefs do not arise as a consequence of being an atheist, they arise as a consequence of being a human (. . . with an ability to feel empathy) and growing up in the presence

103

of other humans." Kiely's point is well taken. I do continue to define atheism as a religion, at least insofar as it helps to frame the atheist's understanding of the reality in which the humane values are held.

Whether or not the religion label fits, there remains the question of whether Christianity has anything to learn from this God-denying view. It's a hard call! And yet, I believe Christians *can* learn from atheism. While disputing the definition, Kiely concludes that "it seems perfectly reasonable to include a chapter (in this book) on what Christians might learn from people who lack any religion."

Thus reassured, I will proceed. This chapter will consider two kinds of atheism: Marxism and a more recent spate of atheistic writings.

Learning from Marxism

Since the dissolution of the Soviet Union in 1991, vast changes in Eastern European countries, and the movement toward capitalism in China and some other former bastions of communism, Marxism seems totally collapsed as a world force in political and economic terms. Given the huge influence of Marxism throughout most of the twentieth century, this is a remarkable turnaround. The influence of Marxism after the Russian Revolution of 1917 was felt well beyond the officially Marxist countries. Reaction to it was experienced in the West in negative form as powerful, sometimes virulent anticommunism. Anything smacking of communist influence was, in the United States, often taken to be subversive, sometimes even as treason.

For several decades, I taught courses on Christianity and Marxism, seeking to help students understand this important world force. I urged students to try to understand Marxism as well as Marxists before endeavoring to criticize. That was put to the test when I invited a leading northern California Communist to speak to a class of undergraduates at the University of the Pacific during the early 1960s. My impression was that a number of the students understood Marxism better than he did—and without themselves becoming Marxists! Interest in such classes abruptly ended around 1990, and it ceased to be high on my own agenda as an ethicist.

I am not so sure that Marxism is now only a fossil. It was hugely important in the lives of hundreds of millions of people through most of the twentieth century, with some lingering echoes. No longer lively as a political force, Marxism might take a place alongside other intellectual and spiritual movements. Liberated from their own political power, so to speak, Marxist ideas are free to be considered on their merits. Those ideas no longer have to be viewed through a prism of communist or anticommunist political orthodoxy. So what about Marxist ideas? Can Christians learn anything from them?

Marxism, beginning with Karl Marx himself during the mid-nineteenth century, was thoroughly atheistic. Marx famously referred to religion as the "opiate of the people." By that he meant that the oppressed masses in a capitalistic society turn to religion as a solace for their social and economic pain. Religion was the heart of a heartless world. The term "opiate of the people" was not entirely negative; the narcotic was not without value. To Marx, it was *needed* by people who had no other recourse. With the new revolutionary possibilities of overcoming the oppressive order, however, the people would no longer need religion. In due course, religion could be expected to "wither away." Having gained power, first in the Soviet Union, then in Eastern Europe, then in China and other countries, Communist parties sought to help religion "wither away." In most such countries, religion remained a legal, though severely disabled, part of society. Many churches were turned into antireligious museums, young people professing religious faith were denied opportunities in higher education, and believers faced discrimination of different kinds. During the years of Communist domination Albania was the only Communist country that treated religion as a punishable crime, but it was stigmatized elsewhere.

The classical Marxist analysis of religion was not limited to its role in buttressing capitalist society. Marx's writings of 1844 probed the spiritual reality more deeply. Human beings are essentially creative. Human creativity is the basis of positive social interactions. We make things (including cultural as well as material products) for their own sake and for the contribution they make to others. The distortion created by capitalism, in Marx's view, is to transform our work from being a creative expression of our humanity into being a product for sale; now it is something outside ourselves. We work for the money we will receive. The buyers of our work have alienated us from our work. We have gained money but, in a sense, we have lost our soul—that is, our essence as human beings. That is true even if we have been richly rewarded in monetary terms. For most people, the money received falls far short of the value created. Thus, for most people, this humanistic alienation is also a kind of wage slavery. Marx puts it this way:

> The worker is related to the *product of his labor* as to an *alien* object. For it is clear according to this premise: The more the worker exerts himself, the more powerful becomes the alien objective world which he fashions against himself, the poorer he and his inner world become, the less there is

that belongs to him. It is the same in religion. The more man attributes to God, the less he retains in himself. . . . The life he has given to the object confronts him as hostile and alien.

Marx originally thought that there would be no need for economic specialization in the coming classless society. He came to understand that there must be division of labor, with different people performing different tasks. Still, alienation would be overcome because life would not be reduced to working for money. Now it would be "from each according to his [or her] ability, to each according to his [or her] need." Would some people respond to such an order by being lazy, letting others do the work? The Marxist analysis is that people are not indolent by nature. We may lose motivation when incentives are abstracted from the reality—that is, when we no longer work for the sake of what we are creating and for the sake of the society we are serving. Basically, we *want* to work, we *want* to create.

Can Christians learn from Marxism? Probably not from its atheism as such. Marxist atheism is a reflection of garden-variety nineteenth-century European atheism, better represented by the twenty-first-century atheists we will turn to below. But there may be more to that concept of alienation in a materialistic society. We are not what we own. We are not what we use. Marx would have appreciated the lines of William Wordsworth's poem "The World Is Too Much with Us" (written in 1806—a dozen years before Marx was born), except he would have defined "the world" more carefully, perhaps recalling his lines about religion as "the heart of a heartless world."

> The world is too much with us; late and soon,
> Getting and spending, we lay waste our powers:
> Little we see in Nature that is ours;
> We have given our hearts away, a sordid boon!

"We have given our hearts away." We cannot know the extent to which Marx was influenced by Christian humanism, but Christians today do well to recover his sense that there is much more to life than the cash nexus.

Even in societies that are predominantly Christian, materialism can seep in. Who of us has not been influenced by materialistic values? Of course, we need to use material things. We need bread, even if we do not live by bread alone. The problem is when we take economic goods as core values, end rather than means to the end. Economic life can be characterized as instrumental, composed of the instruments we use to facilitate the real ends, the intrinsic values through which our true humanity can be realized. We are dehumanized when we turn the intrinsic values, such as love, into mere instruments for material gains, and treat the instrumental as intrinsic.

Illustrations leap to mind. For instance, somebody marries a wealthy person, not out of love but to get rich. Prostitution is an even more obvious illustration, engaging in sex for money, not love, and often with contempt for the client (and for oneself). Or consider a musician who does not compose or perform music for the sake of self-expression but just to make money. Or a writer who cranks out books not to share ideas but just for the money. Or a farmer who grows and harvests crops only for the sale, not for the good that the crops will do and the personal sense of accomplishment. Even closer to Marx's point, consider corporate executives and investors. Do they have a sense of vocation about their work—the good that can be done through useful products and the benefit of workers? Or is the corporation's sole concern making money? That is essentially the problem that Marx raised with his concept of alienation. Christians can gain something from that kind of analysis even when they question Marxism's specific views of economic development. It may occur to many readers that what is at stake here for Christians is the encouragement or loss of a sense of vocation. When we do things for the sake of the good to be accomplished, it is for the benefit of fellow humanity and, Christians believe, for the glory of God.

What about the economic analysis? Is there anything there for Christian social ethics? That analysis is flawed in its dogmatic predictions of periodic economic catastrophes leading to a final breakdown of the whole capitalistic system. History has not been kind to Marxist forecasts at this point, nor to the Marxist failure to anticipate economic adjustments to prevent economic catastrophe. Marxism has neglected the contributions of Keynesian economic theory and the possibilities of a mixed economy.

But before dismissing this movement entirely out of hand, we should remember that its central commitment is to the well-being of whole societies. We can agree with the basic Marxian view that the business of economics is to undergird the ability of *everyone* to participate in the life of the community. That central goal can be lost when the economic well-being of people is left to market forces alone. If flawed Marxian economics has resulted in economic failure in Marxist countries, flawed free-enterprise theory has had the practical effect of destroying the lives of many people as well. There is shrewd insight in the Marxian concept of the "industrial reserve army." In brief, that speaks of the need in a capitalist economy for enough unemployed people to keep wages down, as many workers compete for few jobs. It is in the interest of employers to have more people available than there are positions to be filled, so workers will be content with lower wages. The point has been illustrated in the unemployment crisis of recent years, as it was during the Great Depression of the 1930s and, to a lesser degree, at other times.

I had a chance to see this firsthand during the 1960s in central California. Farmworkers were not included in federal minimum-wage laws, and a *bracero* program brought additional workers from Mexico to the California fields. In effect, these workers were competing with American migrant workers. A number of Christian denominations strongly supported changes in law, and they joined the attempts to organize farmworkers for collective bargaining. A farmer's spouse accosted me about that. "We're doing all we can already to improve wages and living conditions," she protested. But that was exactly the point. Her husband's farm had to compete with others—in particular with the large agribusinesses. As long as labor was treated simply as a cost of doing business and there were no legal or economic protections for workers, those who paid the least had the greatest advantage in the market. Since their labor costs were lower, they could outcompete farmers who paid better wages. So, in effect, the larger-than-needed supply of workers was a "reserve army," as Marx had said.

How do these insights translate into a Christian social ethic? If the foundation of Christian ethics is the unmerited love of God binding us together in a universal moral community, then the economic relationships that make it possible for all to participate in that community are important. Unemployment is a moral issue, not just an economic problem. Sole reliance on a free-market economy to generate enough jobs is not good enough. Under modern conditions, I believe this means that the whole community, the whole society, must provide employment opportunity for those who cannot find work in the private sector. Surely there is much to be done on behalf of the community. Periods of great expansion in American economic life have often been served by such public commitment. Ironically, wartime situations when large numbers of people are "employed" in the armed forces have seen such expansion. World War II effectively ended the Great Depression, and the wise enactment of the GI Bill prevented a return to widespread unemployment.

In addition, a strong case can be made for enlarging the number of economic benefits available to all. Already, it is well established in the United States and other economically advanced countries that education (at least through high school) should be freely available to all. Families don't have to provide for that unless they choose private school as an alternative. Health care for the elderly is also, to a large extent, not a private obligation. Provision of more such benefits can greatly relieve the pressure on all families.

Another facet of Marxism must be raised, however: the shabby political and human rights record of Marxist countries. Stalinist totalitarianism in the

Soviet Union, now thankfully over, remains in North Korea and, to a lesser extent, in a few other countries. A serious blind spot in Marxism was its assumption that the proletariat (working class), once in power, would act in behalf of all people. In a classless society there would be no oppression. Astute Christian observers like Reinhold Niebuhr saw that Marx had failed to take human sinfulness into account. That failure had its roots in the Marxian version of atheism. There was no deep sense of moral accountability. Even a power based on the working class could provide opportunities for corruption and human rights abuses. A Christian respect for God and for the realities of human sinfulness can help prevent such abuses. Indeed, there is a strong Christian case to be made for democracy. Of course, the shabby political and human rights record of Marxist countries cannot be mentioned without remembering that such abuses have also occurred in historically Christian countries. We should not compare the best of Christian expression with the worst of Marxian behavior.

That said, we may need to learn something from the Marxist criticism of the domination of politics by private economic interests. Concentrations of economic wealth can translate into concentrations of political power. Unrestrained economic freedom can become a different, but also unjust, form of oppression. The cure for that is not to follow the Marxist path into revolution and an ephemeral classless society. Rather, it is for the democratic government to regulate and restrain economic forces and for people to hold government itself accountable. The late socialist thinker Michael Harrington made a shrewd observation in his criticism of Stalinism: when government controls the economy, it is important to ask who controls the government.

Twenty-First-Century Atheism

A new crop of atheists has emerged in the latter years of the twentieth century and the early years of the twenty-first. The new atheists are not Marxists; some are, in fact, committed to free-enterprise libertarianism. The most important writers are particularly impressed by what they consider to be the conflict between modern science and any religious worldview. Foremost among them is the British biologist Richard Dawkins, whose best-selling book *The God Delusion* states the case for atheism with great literary skill, holding that atheism does not entail loss of a sense of wonder about the universe, scientifically understood. He writes that an atheist is somebody who believes there is nothing beyond the natural, physical world, no *super*natural creative intelligence lurking behind the observable universe, no soul that outlasts the body and no miracles—except in the sense of natural phenomena that we don't yet understand. If there is something that appears to lie beyond the natural world as it is now imperfectly understood, we hope eventually to understand it and embrace it within the natural. As ever when we unweave a rainbow, it will not become less wonderful.

"Historically," he writes, "religion aspired to *explain* our own existence and the nature of the universe in which we find ourselves. In this role it is now completely superseded by science." Dawkins believes that science has provided an elegant theory of the origin and development of human life and the universe, largely informed by evolutionary theory, specifically the process of natural selection. He does not claim to *know* that there is no God, but puts that on the same level as *knowing* that there are not other kinds of beings, like fairies. Science is based on probabilities, and the probability of God's existence is near zero.

However, Dawkins and other contemporary atheists do not regard religion simply as a scientific or philosophical error. It reinforces narrow-mindedness, obstructing a broader, more wonderful conception of the universe. He quotes, with approval, a passage by the late Carl Sagan:

How is it that hardly any major religion has looked at science and concluded, "This is better than we thought! The Universe is much bigger than our prophets said, grander, more subtle, more elegant"? Instead they say, "No, no, no! My god is a little god, and I want him to stay that way." A religion, old or new, that stressed the magnificence of the Universe as revealed by modern science might be able to draw forth reserves of reverence and awe hardly tapped by the conventional faiths.

Contemporary atheistic writers emphasize the evils that have been spawned in the name of religion. Christopher Hitchens makes that case with some eloquence, drawing on both historical and contemporary illustrations. Here are a few representative quotations from his recent book *God Is Not Great*:

Religion has caused innumerable people not just to conduct themselves no better than others, but to allow themselves permission to behave in ways that would make a brothel-keeper or an ethnic cleanser raise an eyebrow.

People of faith are in their different ways planning your and my destruction, and the destruction of all the hard-won human attainments that I have touched upon.

The level of intensity fluctuates according to time and place, but it can be stated as a truth that religion does not, and in the long run cannot, be content with its own marvelous claims and sublime assurances. It *must* seek to interfere with the lives of nonbelievers, or heretics, or adherents of other faiths. It may speak about the bliss of the next world, but it wants power in this one. This is only to be expected. It is, after all, wholly man-made. And it does not have the confidence in its own various preachings even to allow coexistence between different faiths.

Richard Dawkins takes his scalpel to the Bible itself, offering illustrations of how the Bible records, with approval, actions and attitudes that most people today—including many, if not most, Christians—consider to be morally reprehensible: for instance, the commandment by God to kill all men, women, and children in the conquest of the promised land, with the exception of many of the women who could be used for reproduction. The utter destruction of Jericho and its entire population. The drowning of everybody except Noah and his family in a flood caused by God to eradicate human sinfulness, and then the spectacle of the supposedly moral Noah, in drunken excess, engaged in incest with his two daughters. The wiping out of Sodom and Gomorrah, including turning Lot's wife into a pillar of salt for looking back at the destruction of those cities. Lot's giving his two daughters to be used sexually. And so on. Even the New Testament is not spared. There is Jesus' brusqueness toward his own mother and his insistence that his followers should leave family behind.

Dawkins is especially scathing in his comments about what he considers to be the central doctrine of Christianity, as reflected in the New Testament:

> I have described atonement, the central doctrine of Christianity, as vicious, sado-masochistic and repellent. We should also dismiss it as barking mad, but for its ubiquitous familiarity which has dulled our objectivity. If God wanted to forgive our sins, why not just forgive them, without having Himself tortured and executed in payment—thereby, incidentally, condemning remote future generations of Jews to pogroms and persecution as "Christ-killers."

Dawkins acknowledges that much of the morally objectionable material in the Bible is mythological in character and that many Christians recognize that. But why then, he wonders, should Christians continue to adhere to such myths?

Both Dawkins and Hitchens, along with other contemporary atheists, insist that religion is not necessary for high moral standards and for love of and appreciation for life. As Hitchens puts it, atheists are not immune to the lure of wonder and mystery and awe: we have music and art and literature, and find that the serious ethical dilemmas are better handled by Shakespeare and Tolstoy and Schiller and Dostoyevsky and George Eliot than in the mythical morality tales of the holy books. Literature, not scripture, sustains the mind and—since there is no other metaphor—also the soul. We do not believe in heaven or hell, yet no statistic will ever find that without these blandishments and threats we commit more crimes of greed or violence than the faithful.

Can Christians learn anything from these twenty-first-century atheistic writings and the atheistic movements they represent? It will be difficult to get beyond initial anger and a sense that atheists often overstate their case and distort contemporary Christianity. It is as though the atheists have not heeded the admonition that one should not compare the best of one's own view with the worst of the views one is criticizing! Dawkins briefly approves of the Sermon on the Mount and recalls his positive impression of a school chaplain during his youth, but he does not attend to such biblical gems as Paul's eloquent tribute to love in the thirteenth chapter of First Corinthians. Characterizing even Jesus as concerned only about his own Jewish community, he overlooks the parable of the Good Samaritan and some positive interactions with Roman soldiers. He also omits mention of some of the high points of Old Testament faith, such as Psalms 8 and 23, Isaiah 40, and prophetic writings on universalism, plus the deeply universalistic themes of Jonah and Ruth.

Some years ago, when teaching a seminary class on world religions, I required the students to read Dawkins's *The God Delusion*. Not surprisingly, that book, more than any of the writings from other world religions, almost led to rebellion! But can we indeed learn from such literature?

I believe so. Perhaps the first point is that we can accept a moral and intellectual responsibility to be honest about our faith. We must be devoted to truth, wherever it leads us, as we have also learned from the Zoroastrians—even if that means being brutally frank about the moral and spiritual flaws in our own tradition. That certainly means we must recognize that the Bible contains a good deal of mythological material, and that not all of the myths point in directions we can any longer support. Some may be tempted to say that the Old Testament accounts of genocide reflect divine teaching relevant to the distant past. But could such stories *ever* have represented the will of the God of love whom we worship?

Atheistic writers, such as Hitchens, make much of biblical portraits of God as a jealous God who insists on slavish praise and obedience. A ready

Christian (and Jewish and Muslim) response is that if we do not worship God, we will almost certainly worship a lesser deity. As noted earlier in this book, the ancient Hebrew warnings about idolatry address that point. It is, indeed, tempting to examine the writings of contemporary atheists to ferret out the hidden idols at work there—not least the worship of oneself. But atheists can be people of goodwill who are not self-centered, people who care about justice and who love beauty. Christians do well to ponder the narrower portraits of God that are not at all consistent with one whose spirit is bigger than ours and not at all dependent on flattery from human subjects.

We also do well to take the typical atheist's commitment to science more seriously. Couldn't we agree with Hitchens's comments about science and reason?

> We do not rely solely upon science and reason, because these are necessary rather than sufficient factors, but we distrust anything that contradicts science or outrages reason. We may differ on many things, but what we respect is free inquiry, openmindedness, and the pursuit of ideas for their own sake.

This leads Hitchens to a full-throated assault on religion, anticipated by the subtitle of *God Is Not Great: How Religion Poisons Everything*. He registers these objections:

> There still remain four irreducible objections to religious faith: that it wholly misrepresents the origins of man and the cosmos, that because of this original error it manages to combine the maximum of servility with the maximum of solipsism, that it is both the result and the cause of dangerous sexual repression, and that it is ultimately grounded on wish-thinking.

These are sweeping claims! Nevertheless, the underlying commitment to a scientific worldview is something Christians can learn from.

Science is, after all, the disciplined examination of facts. Truth is surely deeper than the sum of observable fact. But Hitchens's comment that we should "distrust anything that contradicts science or outrages reason" pays tribute to truth and therefore to God the Creator and Source of all truth. Certainly many Christians are open to the disciplines and findings of science and are committed to free inquiry. But far too many Christians reject science and feel threatened by free inquiry. The efforts by numbers of American Christians to push public schools to teach "creation science" are thinly veiled attacks on the well-established theory of evolution. It is one thing to question details in such a theory, thereby improving its accuracy; it is another to dispute well-established, observable fact. It is even more cause for sadness that there remain Christians who insist that the earth was created in 4000 BCE, when the factual evidence points clearly to the world's being several billion years old. Even humanity itself long precedes 4000 BCE. About such matters, thoughtful Christians should not be at all defensive in their interactions with fundamentalist Christians. Surely it is a high responsibility of the Christian pulpit and church school classes to foster respect for truth wherever it leads us.

Atheists push Christians and the adherents of other religions at another point: the tendency to use power to advance their movements and institutions. Every religion strives for cultural expression, and most seek to attract others to their religious views. But when people are directly or even indirectly forced to accept a particular religion, one never knows whether such converts are genuinely persuaded or simply mouthing acceptable views. Of course, atheism itself sometimes has made use of force, as in France in the years following the French Revolution and in the various Marxist countries even more so. As we have noted, in the Soviet Union it was necessary to be a visible Communist for social preferment, such as educational and vocational opportunity—and in some settings, such as Albania and during the Chinese Cultural Revolution, there was outright persecution of members of religions. So how, in those settings, could you tell who was a real Marxist? It was more than interesting to observe the rapidity with which Marxism was abandoned by many people after the breakup of the Soviet Union and the abandonment of official Marxism in satellite states. Religion is at its best when it relies on persuasion, not on force.

The Christian-Marxist dialogues in Czechoslovakia during the 1960s brought out the best in both movements precisely because of the mutual respect in a climate of openness. That kind of dialogue was one of the factors leading to the Czech movement known internationally as the Prague Spring. Unfortunately, that honest effort to create "socialism with a human face" came to an abrupt end when the USSR and other Communist countries invaded Czechoslovakia in August 1968. This was a huge tragedy. I visited Czechoslovakia during the summer of 1969 when many of the winds of freedom still blew and experienced the deep disillusionment of many Czechs. Years later, the Velvet Revolution provided new opportunity for that spirit to manifest itself in that country.

Perhaps the larger point here is that fresh winds of the spirit are ill served by slavish adherence to conventional wisdom, particularly when the latter relies on social pressure and the power of the state. Christ on the cross had more influence on the course of history than any of the Caesars. Atheists like

Richard Dawkins and Christopher Hitchens are not much impressed by this way of putting it, but they help us see how the use of force and social pressure undermine both our quest for truth and our embrace of values.

They can also help us resist taking cheap shots at atheists, particularly when we insist that morality depends on belief in God. While Christians and the adherents of most other religions understand that our moral life is closely related to what we ultimately believe to be good and true, it is unfair to characterize all atheists as lacking such a center of value. Indeed, sometimes atheists continue to find value in religious traditions they no longer accept literally. As one illustration of this, Elisabeth Cornwell wrote an intriguing article in the *Washington Post* a few days before Christmas in 2011:

> When people find out I'm an atheist, the question often comes up about what I do during the Christmas holidays. There is an assumption that atheists don't "do Christmas," so they are surprised when I say how much I love it. . . .
>
> Families and friends are what create the celebration of the season. . . . We can see how celebration is truly a human phenomenon, independent of religion. I feel no sense of hypocrisy because I enjoy the many threads of my familial past. Nor do I shy away from singing the familiar and much loved Christmas songs that I sang for years in choir or at home. Silent Night still can bring a tear to my eye because it recalls memories of childhood. . . .
>
> Christmas belongs to anyone who wants it, and just because I gave up believing in a god doesn't mean I gave up believing in the love and joy of family.

Christians can be expected to take a step beyond this, of course. But faith in God does not mean that Christians must question the integrity and moral sensitivity of people who do not share that faith.

An ironic contribution of atheism to persons of religious faith came out during a presentation of an early version of this chapter to a church study group. A ninety-one-year-old man in the group remarked that "atheism is to religion as zero is to mathematics." What on earth do you mean by that? I asked. Zero, he replied, is essential to the whole scheme of numbers. His point was that atheism reinforces religious belief by sharpening the contrast between belief and its absence. I suppose by such logic we could say that sin contributes to morality by the same kind of contrast! We might not want to put it quite like that, but we can agree that morality would be meaningless if we did not have the freedom to be immoral. Atheism helps to clarify the point that we do not have to believe. So religious faith really does mean something. I thank Walter Wells for contributing this insight.

Learning from Albert Einstein

Albert Einstein has been claimed by atheists and by believers in God. The views in his writings on religion are worth mentioning in this chapter, because the great physicist was also a penetrating thinker on morality and religion. He makes clear that he does not believe in a personal God. Theism, to him, means belief in a God who manipulates events, which he considers irrational. But that does not lead Einstein to reject religion. In that respect, he does not exemplify the atheism of Dawkins or Hitchens. He writes eloquently of the dependence of science on a different kind of religious faith:

> Science can only be created by those who are thoroughly imbued with the aspiration towards truth and understanding. This source of feeling, however, springs from the sphere of religion. To this there also belongs the faith in the possibility that the regulations valid for the world of existence are rational, that is, comprehensible to reason. I cannot conceive of a genuine scientist without that profound faith. The situation may be expressed by an image: Science without religion is lame, religion without science is blind.

His objection to what may be a more typical expression of religion is that for there to be an omnipotent God, "every occurrence, including every human action, every human thought, and every human feeling and aspiration is also His work; how is it possible to think of holding men responsible for their deeds and thoughts before such an almighty Being?"

Many Christian thinkers have concluded that God has chosen *not* to manipulate human life and the natural course of things. Is it possible that God should be available to humanity through a divine-human relationship that does not entail such determinism? An analogy might be the relationship between human beings who influence one another spiritually and rationally, but not through physical force. That would also be a form of theism, but not as characterized by Einstein. Nevertheless, this formidable mind has put the case that whatever we think about God, human freedom and the laws governing nature must be respected. I know of no writing by Einstein that encourages prayer, but he certainly has excluded prayers of petition asking God to intervene in a physical way. It may be another matter whether there is a divine spirit at work that can inspire us to act toward divine ends.

So Einstein's religious views cannot be considered either clearly atheistic or clearly religious in the traditional sense. But, almost as a postscript to a consideration of what Christians can learn from atheism, those views are worth pondering.

Questions for Discussion

1. Is atheism really a religion? Does this chapter belong in this book?
2. Can we learn anything from Marx without becoming Marxists?
3. Are there ways in which religion is used to exploit people?
4. Can we take scripture seriously without taking it literally? How are we to deal with inconsistencies in the Bible?
5. Are there aspects of Christian tradition that exhibit cruelty?
6. Is belief in God consistent with science?

Chapter 10

Can Other Religions Learn from Christianity?

*Let love be genuine; hate what is evil, hold fast to what is good;
love one another with mutual affection; outdo one another in showing honor. . . . Rejoice in hope, be patient in suffering, persevere in
prayer. . . . Extend hospitality to strangers.*

—Romans 12:9–13

I have sought in these pages to make and illustrate a central point: Christians
can and should learn from other religions. Some of the learning comes in the
form of new insight, some in fresh interpretations of doctrines already held,
some in reinforcing aspects of Christian faith that have been neglected. I have
not written as an expert on all the religions discussed here, but I have studied
and consulted widely enough to feel confident that the various learnings are
valid. I trust that others will continue and deepen this conversation.

In this chapter, I want to raise a question that many Christian readers are
perhaps itching to have discussed: Granted that we can learn from others,
can they also learn from us? I do not raise this question competitively. This
chapter is not intended to convert anybody from another religion! Indeed,
I would be happy if books might appear by writers from other faiths about
what their religions can learn from faiths other than their own. That will not
happen in any religious context where people are convinced of the absolute
truth of their views and certain that they have nothing to learn from others.
But, as we have seen, there are people in all the religions we have been considering who are not so narrow-minded. So what can other religions learn
from Christianity?

Through the centuries, we've made our share of mistakes, from which
others can learn and already have learned. Most of those have centered on
efforts to use force to propagate the faith or to sustain its cultural power.
External rewards have been used to achieve the same goals. There have been

subtle corruptions of spirit as some Christian leaders seem to have forgotten that Jesus came to serve, not to be served. A fair amount of infighting has occurred between and among Christian denominations, symbolized by the exclusion of fellow Christians from the sacrament of Communion on the grounds that they aren't Christian enough. Doubtless there are many parallels of such mistakes in other religions, but perhaps Christian failings at such points can lead to useful introspection within other faiths.

The Significance of Jesus

Apart from these negative lessons, there are huge positives. Take Jesus himself. Holding Jesus in high regard does not in itself require conversion—Mohandas Gandhi is but one illustration of adherents of other religions who have been greatly influenced by Jesus without necessarily becoming Christians. The Qur'an provides evidence that Muslims, far from despising or even neglecting Jesus, number him among the greatest of God's prophets and messengers.

To Christians, Jesus is not simply a great teacher—although he is that. He lived on earth as a man of huge spiritual depth, a spirit overflowing with love. The Gospel narratives about his life vary, to be sure. But central to all of them is his willingness to die the cruel, tortured, and humiliating death of a Roman crucifixion. The only escape available to him, which he rejected, was the renunciation of his central vision of the love of God. But Jesus' death, though a kind of martyrdom, was more than the courageous martyrdom of a Socrates. His death was more than a display of courage; it was an act of love. It did not occur for the sake of his personal integrity nor any other personal benefit. It was for the sake of others, and so it has registered among Christians through the ages. People everywhere can learn from that embodiment of love.

In his writings, the apostle Paul treats the cross as the most important symbol of the faith because it expresses what he calls grace. That term, taken from a Roman legal context, refers to setting aside a deserved punishment. Some Christians have, in my opinion, applied this too mechanically by treating it as God setting aside our deserved punishments for sin. There is a deeper meaning: God's love for us can be counted on despite our imperfections. In this sense God is not a stern judge softening up a bit because of Jesus. Rather, God loves us, each one, even beyond our comprehension and despite our moral flaws. Religions that tend to portray the divine-human relationship in legal terms can learn something about loving relationship as being more basic than any law. The law exists to serve such relationships.

Does this mean that what we do no longer matters? Is this what the martyred German theologian Dietrich Bonhoeffer called "cheap grace"? Hardly, for one cannot receive love unlovingly. Voltaire is alleged to have said, "Oh, God will forgive. That's his business." Yes, indeed; to Christians it certainly *is* God's business. But such cynicism is wide of the mark. Put it this way: We can count on God's love, regardless of what we say or do. But we must not put barriers in the way. Isn't that also true in human relationships? A parent may love a child totally, without limit. But while resisting that love, the child cannot receive it. In time, there may come a breakthrough. Something can happen to make the parent's love crystal clear, enabling the child to enter fully into the loving relationship.

Interpretation of Scripture

Most of the religions discussed in these pages have scriptures that are considered to be sacred. The question *why* scriptures are sacred is obviously crucial. If scriptures are believed to be dictated directly by God (or another divine source), there may still be some room for interpretation—such as, what did God really *mean* by this or that commandment? That is even more the case when it is believed, as it is by some Muslims, that God intended part of the scripture to be understood as true and binding for all time and part as a message that applied only during the age in which the message was delivered; that is, scripture is partly timeless and partly time bound and relative to a particular cultural setting.

Even if all scripture is considered timeless, the human beings who read and apply it are not infallible. Even those who believe that the Bible or the Qur'an is absolutely and universally true must accept that human beings are not God. People can be mistaken in their understanding of scripture.

The variabilities of language have to be considered as well. Words are not always instruments of precision. They grow out of cultural experience and are capable of different, sometimes conflicting, meanings. I can understand, therefore, why Muslims insist that the Qur'an cannot be fully grasped except in the original Arabic language. Christians who are biblical literalists generally say that the Bible is without error, but only in its original writing. Regrettably, none of the original manuscripts exist. The teachings of Jesus were in Aramaic, and we don't have his words recorded in Aramaic—only as translated into Greek and subsequently into English and other languages.

What might other religions learn from Christians about the uses of scripture? Christian biblical scholars over the past two hundred years have refined the study of the Bible with much art and skill. The probable dates and cultural settings of the different writings have been probed endlessly, often with scholarly disagreements. For instance, the dates of some of the Gospels can be fixed more accurately by reference to known historical events that are not assumed by the writers—or by reference to events reflected in the writings. Moreover, there is greater knowledge now of the process of canonization—that is, of deciding which writings should be treated as sacred and which do not rise to that level. In short, the study of Christian Scripture has become much more sophisticated. Has this diminished the spiritual import of the Bible? To the contrary, it has probably drawn us into deeper awareness of what is important and what is not.

I am aware that scriptures of other religions have been approached with great scholarly care through the years—even through the centuries. Still, some of the specific methods employed by Christian biblical scholars might well be utilized by adherents of other faiths without diminishing the importance of their own sacred writings, and without their having to become Christians.

Theological and Ethical Thinking

Similarly, Christian thought through the past two millennia has contributed ways of grasping religious truth that can contribute to other faith traditions. My own field is Christian ethics. I think and write as a Christian. But my approach to the ethical meaning of the Christian faith has been helped greatly by methods of analysis that can be appropriated easily by persons of other faith traditions. For example, twentieth-century ethicists have contributed insight into three forms of ethical thought: The prescriptive approach (which ethicists call deontological) thinks of ethics in legal terms—laws, rules, principles. The operational or consequentialist approach focuses on the good to be sought and the means necessary to gain the good. The relational approach focuses on human relationships and our relationships to God, the world, and other sentient beings; the supreme focus is on love. Obviously each of these three can be helpful, but much depends on which of the three is taken as the main framework. I use this as one illustration of the kinds of thinking that generations of Christian thinkers have refined. I'll add my own twist here: As we sort out the problems and dilemmas of real life, seeking to be faithful to our deepest values, we often can be helped by deciding where to place the burden of proof. When in doubt, how shall we proceed?

Twentieth-century Christian theologians have helped us better understand the significance of social institutions—political, economic, familial. The

American theologian Reinhold Niebuhr wrote persuasively about how people can be very good in their personal lives while unconsciously supporting oppressive social institutions on a wider scale. Before him, Walter Rauschenbusch expressed a similar insight in his definition of a Christianized society as a society where bad people are forced to do good things. By contrast, an unchristian society is one in which good people are forced to do bad things. I don't much like the term "Christianized society," and I cannot imagine it being attractive to people of other religions. But consider: in a society governed by unjust systems, everybody has to act unjustly by living normal lives. By contrast, when laws and institutions support human rights, even people who do not care about others must act with justice and fairness. I could see that kind of insight being used in societies where religions other than Christianity are dominant.

Learning from the Secular Enlightenment

How should religions think about the Enlightenment—the intellectual and cultural developments of (roughly) the seventeenth and eighteenth centuries? It included major scientific advances, such as those identified with Isaac Newton, and philosophical movements associated with such figures as Thomas Hobbes, John Locke, and Jean-Jacques Rousseau. On the whole, it was a burst of secular thought, even though a number of its principal figures thought of themselves as Christians. There is a tendency in some Christian circles to believe that the Enlightenment was, on the whole, a wrong direction for Christians.

But that may be too simple. Some Enlightenment thought was indeed contrary to Christian faith. For instance, Voltaire and Rousseau were explicitly opposed to the church. That is not true of Locke or Newton, or such philosophers as Immanuel Kant or Adam Smith. There are Christian thinkers who consider the Enlightenment to be wrongheaded because it was essentially individualistic. One can identify individualistic aspects in the thought of Locke and Kant. On the other hand, Rousseau was profoundly social in his understanding of the social contract by which we are all bound.

I raise the question of the Enlightenment because of its great influence on twentieth-century Christian theology, particularly in its Protestant form. That influence has included respect for and use of the natural and social sciences, commitment to democracy and human rights and equality of all persons before the law, and use of secular philosophy in the work of theology. In short, the Enlightenment has encouraged the pursuit of truth, wherever it can be found, and a heightened sense of the worth of all persons. Christian theology is not diminished by such commitments. For example, the sciences have contributed immeasurably to our understanding of the physical world and its setting in the universe. Science is not itself about God. But it helps believers in God as the source and sustainer of all that is to better understand what God has done and is doing. Philosophy is not the same thing as theology, but it can help guard theology from logical errors and unreasonable truth claims. The behavioral sciences, later offshoots of the Enlightenment, help us better understand why people do what they do.

A number of the religions discussed in this book are also grappling with secular intellectual and scientific developments. I believe that much is to be learned from Christian experience with these developments over the past two or three centuries.

Christian Engagement with Political Life

Most religions have been involved in politics, sometimes by reinforcing the authority of political institutions and rulers, often by being subservient to secular rulers, occasionally as a force for change. In tribal cultures there has often been unity of political and spiritual powers. Even more complex civilizations have sometimes been theocratic, with religious leadership dominating public policy. So Christian experience with politics is not unique.

Still, Christians have developed ways of affecting political life that can be studied by other faiths. The American civil rights movement is one illustration. Initially led by a handful of Christian leaders, such as the Revs. Martin Luther King Jr. and Ralph Abernathy, the movement sought to overcome long-standing racial segregation in the quest for what King called the beloved community. The movement eschewed violence and showed respect for the humanity of its opponents, even while resisting the oppressive laws and institutions the opponents represented. One of the reasons for the movement's success was the social and political support it received from Christian organizations. Centuries earlier, Quakers and Methodists (among others) played a central role in ending the slave trade and ultimately slavery itself. Today, American Christian churches seek to affect public policies on a wide variety of issues, most notably dealing with economic distress, environmental problems, and health care. A number of Christian denominations have boards or committees specifically authorized to advocate for policies reflecting the churches' ethical insights.

Of course, Christians are not always in agreement about public policies. Two of the most divisive issues in America are whether abortion should be sanctioned by law and whether same-gender unions should be recognized as marriage. These issues, and the earlier question of prohibition of alcoholic beverages, have pressed us to decide how far the state should go in enforcing moral views that are peculiar to particular religious groups. Should those who do not subscribe to a church's moral teaching be compelled by law to follow those teachings? Some legal thinkers have argued that this should not be done unless there is also a clear secular purpose for a given law—as there clearly is in such a case as the prohibition of racial discrimination by businesses serving the public.

I believe persons of other religions can benefit from study of how Christians have struggled with such issues—particularly adherents of religions in countries where their faith is dominant and the temptation is present to deny religious freedom to members of religious minorities.

Christian Ecumenism

Finally, Christian ecumenical movements may provide helpful insights for non-Christian religions. Christian ecumenicity was born out of centuries of deep and sometimes bloody conflict following the Protestant Reformation of the sixteenth century. Deep animosity between Roman Catholic and Protestant Christians continued until the latter part of the twentieth century. Meanwhile, Protestant denominations competed among themselves vigorously. Greater cooperation began during the nineteenth century, partly prompted by nondenominational movements, such as the YMCA and Student Volunteer Movement, in which Protestants sought to work together for common objectives across denominational lines. The Life and Work and the Faith and Order movements in the early twentieth century developed into the World Council of Churches in 1948, an organization that came to include Eastern Orthodoxy as well. Similar councils of churches were created in other countries. The story is much too long to be detailed here, but other religions have learned from this, sometimes copying institutional forms. Panreligious organizations have been partly modeled on these ecumenical lines. Christian ecumenism itself received a major boost with the Second Vatican Council of the Roman Catholic Church during the 1960s.

All of the major world religions, and most of the smaller ones as well, include different, sometimes competing, groups or denominations. Some examples are the Shia and Sunni Muslim groups, with various subsets, and the Mahayana and Theravada forms of Buddhism—also with many subsets. Differences within and beyond the various religions are not always easily overcome. The Christian experience certainly evidences that. But much is to be gained by efforts corresponding, more or less, to the Christian ecumenical movement. Overcoming differences within a religion is a major step toward better relationships among religions. Toward that end, other religions can learn practical lessons from Christian ecumenical movements.

Conclusion

I must repeat that I have not, in this concluding chapter, sought to suggest that other religions should simply become Christian. Adherents of the various faiths will doubtless continue to welcome converts, but that is not what this book has been about. We need to *learn* from one another, even as we retain our own basic commitments. I welcome writings by persons in other religions that explore what they can learn from religions other than their own. And I hope this small book will prompt further thought by Christians on what we can learn from others.

Questions for Discussion

1. When we are open to learning from other religions, does that strengthen or weaken our faith as Christians?
2. Should Christian churches still send out missionaries?
3. Which findings of modern science support traditional Christian views? Which seem to be opposed?
4. What do you think interreligious relations will look like a hundred years from now?

In Summary

Fifty Points to Consider

In the foregoing chapters, I have sought to identify points at which Christians can learn from other religions. Some of these represent new insights, at least for many Christians. Others reflect aspects of the Christian tradition that need new emphasis. Still others represent where misunderstandings of Christian faith are brought into focus by other faith traditions. I offer here a concluding summary of the main points in those preceding chapters to sharpen the focus on these ideas and to reinforce that this book is about what we can learn *from* other religions and not just what we can learn *about* those religions.

1. We must not compare the *best* of our own faith to the *worst* in others. Christians should not dismiss the jihad of Muslims as violent conquest while considering Christian Crusades as nonviolent campaigns for some good objective—and vice versa. (Chaps. 1, 3)

2. The Christian view of Christ as the way to God can be interpreted through the love of Christ as a manifestation of the love of God, so that love—not exclusive adherence to Christianity—is the way to God. That love is also to be found in other religions. (Chap. 1)

3. It is possible to remain committed to one's own faith and still learn from others. (Chap. 1)

4. If "religion" means the beliefs and values that are central or ultimate in our lives, then religion comes in many cultural forms, including those that have no place for God. (Chap. 1)

5. The term "revelation" refers to aspects of experience that bring all of life into focus. (Chap. 1)

6. What we worship is central to who we are. (Judaism)

7. The material universe and human history are to be affirmed. (Judaism, Islam)

8. To be "chosen" by God is to be charged with special responsibility; it is not an exclusive privilege. (Judaism)

9. Tradition is indispensable in the transmission of faith from one generation to the next, and myth is an important way of conveying truth. (Judaism)

10. Ordinary adherents to a faith tradition are often more open than theologians. (Islam and others)

11. It is important to accept the value of other religions. (Emphasized by several religions)

12. The monotheism of Christian faith needs greater clarity. The doctrine of the Trinity cannot be understood as three different gods, but rather as three ways in which the one God has been experienced. (Chap. 4)

13. The Muslim view that Muhammad is to be venerated but not worshiped as God can help us see that while we worship the God who is disclosed through Christ, that is not the same as worship of the man Jesus. (Islam)

14. Scientific study should be celebrated, not rejected. (Islam, atheism)

15. Moral and spiritual disciplines are important in spiritual development. (Islam, Asian religions)

16. Nobody has all the answers. The whole of being is beyond human comprehension, even though we all have knowledge of part of it. (Asian religions)

17. God is bigger than any human conception. God encompasses everything, and every aspect of reality gains its significance in relation to God. (Hinduism)

18. We cannot escape responsibilities by retreating into religion. (Hinduism, Buddhism)

19. Spiritual life advances through stages; we cannot become spiritually mature all at once. (Hinduism)

20. Division of labor and of responsibilities is built into the human condition, but those who are among the elite have special responsibility for the weaker and more vulnerable members of society. (Hinduism)

21. Evil, while real, does not have independent existence. (Hinduism)

22. In speaking about God we must not turn God into an abstraction or an object. (Buddhism, atheism)

23. Religious authority figures and scriptures should not be considered to be beyond question or criticism. (Buddhism, Hinduism, atheism)

24. It is an illusion to think of wealth, fame, and power as permanent. (Buddhism, Hinduism)

25. Much human suffering is the result of inordinate craving. (Buddhism)

26. Compassion is the best expression of our humanity. (Buddhism)

27. All our actions, good and bad, have consequences, or Karma. (Buddhism, Hinduism)

28. God should not be given a limiting name. Human names for God point toward God but cannot express the whole reality of God. (Taoism)

29. Excessive competition, dividing humanity into winners and losers, is a prime source of conflict. We should not put ourselves before others. (Taoism)

30. Even if considered to be necessary, war is always tragic. (Taoism)

31. Rulers should govern quietly, without ostentation, not relying primarily on force. (Taoism, Confucianism)

32. Ceremony, religious and otherwise, has limited value. (Taoism)

33. Civility and courtesy are to be prized in political life. (Confucianism)

34. The natural world has spiritual significance. (Primal religions)

35. All of life is interconnected. (Primal religions)

36. Nonviolence, including respect for nonhuman forms of life, is a transcendently important value. (Jainism)

37. People who convert to other religions should not be ostracized. (Jainism)

38. God is present in each of us. (Sikhism, Hinduism)

39. Women must be valued and treated as equal to men. (Sikhism)

40. Commitment to truth should be as close to absolute as possible. (Zoroastrianism)

41. The oneness and unity of humanity is to be affirmed. (Baha'i)

42. Religion should not be used as a substitute for needed social change. (Marxist atheism)

43. Human work and creativity are an expression of our humanity. The product of our work is not simply an objective commodity. (Marxist atheism)

44. A social ethic should lead to commitment by society to ensure employment opportunity and a living wage for all of its members. (Marxist atheism)

45. The Bible contains self-contradictions that cannot be explained away. (Twenty-first-century atheism)

46. There is a dark side to Christian history and tradition, including depictions of a vengeful God, that cannot be accepted morally. (Twenty-first-century atheism)

47. Religion must not be promulgated by compulsion. (Twenty-first-century atheism)

Then, these points where others can learn from Christianity:

48. Grace is prior to law. Unless people feel accepted by God and others, they will be prone to be self-serving.

49. The mainline Christian disciplines of biblical scholarship over the past two centuries can be utilized in other religious traditions. Honest scriptural scholarship enhances religious faith.

50. Twentieth-century mainline Christian ecumenical movements have pioneered disciplines of interdenominational and interfaith relationships from which other religions could learn.

Notes and Sources

Where possible, I have relied on primary sources—that is, the sacred writings or scriptures of the religions discussed in this book. The various religions view their scriptures differently. In some cases, the writings are attributed to direct divine inspiration. In other cases, they are the writings of acknowledged spiritual leaders that have taken on unique authority in the religious tradition. I cannot claim familiarity with the original languages in which these primary sources were written, relying instead on widely accepted English translations.

There are many interpretative writings on the world religions. I want to call special attention to Huston Smith's classic work, *The World's Religions,* 2nd ed. (New York: HarperCollins, 1991). Studies by Karen Armstrong, Diana Eck, and Charles A. Kimball have greatly helped Christians and others in the West better to understand religious traditions other than their own, fostering a healthy appreciation of religious diversity. Many volumes published by Orbis Press have similarly contributed to greater mutual understanding. Of these, I am particularly impressed by Hans Küng, Josef van Ess, Heinrich von Stietencron, and Heinz Bechert, *Christianity and World Religions: Paths to Dialogue* (Maryknoll, NY: Orbis, 1993), a volume containing extensive written dialogues between Küng and experts on Islam, Hinduism, and Buddhism.

While Internet sources must always be used with care, because not all are subjected to careful screening, they can be helpful in identifying figures and dates. Official home pages of several of the religions referred to in this book are quite useful, bearing in mind that they may reflect particular religious subgroups in competition with others. There is no substitute for reading the primary sources, even if that cannot be done in the original languages. For example, I would not be comfortable in relying on interpretations of Islam if I had not read the Qur'an, nor of Buddhism without reference to the Dhammapada or the Lotus Sutra.

CHAPTER 1: LEARNING FROM OTHER RELIGIONS

Biblical quotations in this book are from the New Revised Standard Version, copyright 1989 by the Division of Christian Education of the National Council of Churches in the United States of America.

Omid Safi's words are from his book *Memories of Muhammad: Why the Prophet Matters* (New York: HarperCollins, 2009), 25, 26–27.

The Laymen's Foreign Missions Inquiry project is reported in Commission of Appraisal, *Re-Thinking Missions: A Laymen's Inquiry after One Hundred Years* (New York: Harper & Brothers, 1932).

For the views of Hendrik Kraemer, see his books *The Christian Message in a Non-Christian World* (London: Edinburgh House Press, 1947) and *Religions and the Christian Faith* (Philadelphia: Westminster, 1957).

The Edward Harrison book quoted is *Masks of the Universe: Changing Ideas on the Nature of the Cosmos*, 2nd ed. (Cambridge: Cambridge University Press, 2003), 305–6, 308.

The discussion of revelation in this chapter is partly influenced by the philosopher Edgar S. Brightman's view that "comprehensive coherence" can best help us discern what is true. I find this helpful, but only up to a point. Truth lies in the unification of our understandings of reality. I believe that Brightman erred in describing coherence as the sum total of our knowledge from all sources. I believe some aspects of experience must have greater weight than others in bringing reality into focus. I have dealt with these issues more fully in my *Faith and Fragmentation*, 2nd ed. (Louisville, KY: Westminster John Knox Press, 2004).

CHAPTER 2: LEARNING AFRESH FROM PRIMAL ROOTS

The John Collier quotation that heads this chapter is from Smith's *World Religions*, 382.

Primal religion is undoubtedly the oldest of all religious tendencies; historically it has been present on all the continents (except Antarctica, of course). As I have noted, written sacred texts for primal religions are not available. The beliefs have been transmitted orally through accepted stories and myths. In this section I have relied on secondary accounts, such as Smith's *World Religions* and Jefferson Labala's *Through African Eyes: Biblical Parallel to African Religion and Culture and Its Implications for a New Theological Paradigm* (Long Island City, NY: Seaburn Publishing Group, 2009). Anthropologists have also contributed greatly to our understanding of primal religion, although most such literature refracts these spiritual traditions through Western eyes.

CHAPTER 3: LEARNING FROM JUDAISM

It has become customary in many Christian circles to substitute the name "Hebrew Bible" for "Old Testament," because the term "Old" Testament seems to suggest that it has been superseded by the New Testament. But "old" does not necessarily mean outdated or obsolete. Indeed, some things are valued exactly *because* they are old! The more traditional way of speaking about what we have called the Old Testament itself pays tribute to the immensity of the influence of those writings on Jesus and the earliest Christians. So, with all due respect to those who want to change this way of speaking, I will continue to refer to the first thirty-nine books of the Christian Bible as the Old Testament. Moreover, the Old Testament is not the only writing treated as scriptural by Jews, for the Talmud also enjoys something of that status.

Thomas Cahill's words are from his *The Gifts of the Jews: How a Tribe of Desert Nomads Changed the Way Everyone Thinks and Feels* (New York: Doubleday, 1998).

For a detailed analysis of the influence of the Old Testament on New Testament writings, see Hans Hübner, "New Testament Interpretation of the Old Testament," in Magne Saebo, ed., *Hebrew Bible/Old Testament: The History of Its Interpretation* (Gottingen: Vandenhoeck & Ruprecht, 1996). Hübner writes, "It is fundamental that the New Testament authors read the Scripture of Israel almost unanimously as the written fixing of the word of God who used this very word to announce the act of salvation in Jesus Christ" (p. 337). We should note that the Old Testament writings reflected in the New Testament were largely from the Greek Septuagint translation—not from the original Hebrew.

Arthur Hertzberg's writing is from his *Jews: The Essence and Character of a People* (San Francisco: HarperSanFrancisco, 1998), 29, 19, 22, and 128. The awful quotation from Luther is not consistent with his deeper exposition of the Christian doctrine of grace.

The suggestion that some of the Old Testament traditions, such as those about Abraham, Isaac, and Moses, are more myth than fact is offered by Israel Finkelstein and Neil Asher Silberman, *Bible Unearthed: Archaeology's New Vision of Ancient Israel and the Origins of Its Sacred Texts* (New York: Simon & Schuster, 2001). Their well-documented conclusions will come as a shock to many Christian (and Jewish) readers, as they did to me. Whether or not all those conclusions are ultimately accepted by archaeologists and biblical scholars, they remind us that myth can contain important truth. A truthful myth is better than a misunderstood fact. Karen Armstrong's book *A Short History of Myth* (New York: Canongate, 2005) is a helpful survey of the different forms of myth that have developed from earliest evidences of human culture to the present.

CHAPTER 4: LEARNING FROM ISLAM

The quotation at the head of this chapter is from the N. J. Dawood translation, *The Koran*, rev. ed. (London: Penguin Books, 1999). Other quotations from the Qur'an, unless otherwise noted, are from the translation by Tarif Khalidi, first published in 2008 by the Penguin Group. The original language of the Qur'an was Arabic. Many Muslims consider the Arabic original to be the only truly authentic version of the Qur'an. Since I am unable to read Arabic, I must trust English translations to convey the essence of the parts of the Qur'an that I use. I have consulted with Arabic-speaking Muslim scholars, while noting how other Muslim writers have interpreted key passages. For our purposes in finding points at which Christians can learn from Islam, the different translations are quite similar.

The Qur'an, like the Bible, is divided into chapters, called suras, and I have cited these in the text. Thus 3:84–85 refers to Sura 3, verses 84–85.

"The Quran granted women inheritance rights," and so on, is from Maher Hathout et al., *In Pursuit of Justice: The Jurisprudence of Human Rights in Islam* (Los Angeles: Muslim Public Affairs Council, 2006), 168.

Qur'anic quotations under the heading "Muslim Acceptance of Other Religions" are from the Dawood translation. This translation does not differ substantially from the others, but I believe it presents the issue of monotheism more sharply. The updated translation by Abdullah Yusuf Ali is in *The Meaning of the Holy Qur'an*, 11th ed. (Beltsville, MD: Amana Publications, 2009). This English translation of the Qur'an is greatly preferred by one of my Muslim consultants, partly because it places the English and Arabic versions side by side.

The Ayoub quotation is from Irfan A. Omar, ed., *A Muslim View of Christianity: Essays on Dialogue by Mahmoud Ayoub* (Maryknoll, NY: Orbis Books, 2007), 14.

Qur'anic quotations under the heading "The Challenge of Islamic Monotheism" and quotations from the Qur'an at the head of this chapter are from the Dawood translation.

The proper name for Avicenna, who lived from 980 to 1037, is Ibn Sina, and Averroes, who lived from 1126 to 1198, is properly known as Ibn Rushd.

The Menocal references are from María Rosa Menocal, *The Ornament of the World: How Muslims, Jews, and Christians Created a Culture of Tolerance in Medieval Spain* (Boston: Little, Brown, & Co., 2002). Her summary comment is at p. 277. The quote from Harold Bloom is on p. xv.

The letter from Pope Gregory VII is cited in *Nostra Aetate* (Declaration on the Relation of the Church to Non-Christian Religions), issued by Pope Paul VI in 1965. See J. Neuner, SJ, and J. Dupuis, SJ, eds., *The Christian Faith in the Doctrinal Documents of the Catholic Faith* (Bangalore: Theological Publications in India, 1973).

Feisal Abdul Rauf's book is *What's Right with Islam Is What's Right with America* (New York: HarperCollins, 2004). The quotation is from p. 129.

Ranya Idliby, Suzanne Oliver, and Priscilla Warner wrote *The Faith Club: A Muslim, a Christian, a Jew—Three Women Search for Understanding* (New York: Simon & Schuster, 2006).

The Rumi quotations are from Kabir Helminski, ed., *The Rumi Collection* (Boston: Shambhala Classics, 2000). Background on the life of Rumi and the Sufi movement is from the foreword to this book and from Wikipedia articles.

CHAPTER 5: LEARNING FROM HINDUISM

Hindu sacred writings are ancient, vast, and complex. In this chapter I have relied principally on the Bhagavad Gita, the Uddhava Gita, and some of the Upanishads. The Gitas depict Krishna, who ultimately represents Brahman, in dialogue with Uddhava and Prince Arjuna. These writings, particularly the Bhagavad Gita, are extraordinary contributions to literature, apart from their religious significance. Quotations from the Bhagavad Gita are, with one exception, from the Juan Mascaró translation (London: Penguin Classics, 1962). Quotations from the Uddhava Gita are from Swami Ambikananda Saraswati, trans., *The Uddhava Gita: The Final Teaching of Krishna* (Berkeley, CA: Seastone, 2002). The Upanishads quotations are from Eknath Easwaran, trans., *The Upanishads* (Tomales, CA: Nilgiri Press, 2007).

The Julius Lipner quotation is from his *Hindus: Their Religious Beliefs and Practices* (London: Routledge, 1998), 6.

"The Supreme Personality of Godhead . . ." is from the translation by A. C. Bhaktivedanta Prabhupada in *Bhagavad Gita As It Is,* 2nd ed. (London: The Bhaktivedanta Book Trust, 1983), selections taken from 10:19–42.

In the section called "Reality and Illusion": Uddhava Gita 5.33–35; *Katha Upanishad* 10; Bhagavad Gita 5.20–21, 7.24–25, 7.27, 13.9.

In the section titled "Human Fulfillment": Uddhava Gita 17.50, 51, 56; *Shvetashvatara Upanishad* 2.5–7, 1.2.1–2; Bhagavad Gita 6.20–22, 12.2, 12.4, 11.54, 12.18, 3.4, 3.8; *Taittiriya Upanishad* 2.5.1, 8.1, 9.1, 10.1–4.

The Hindu friend quoted in this chapter is D. C. Rao, a leader among Washington, DC, Hindus.

In the section on the caste system: *Brihad-Aranyaka Upanishad* 4.22; *Mundaka Upanishad* 1.1.6; Uddhava Gita 12.20; Bhagavad Gita 13.28, 16.1–3.

In the section "Hindu Beliefs about Evil": Uddhava Gita 14, 23, 22.

CHAPTER 6: LEARNING FROM BUDDHISM

I have relied on the Dhammapada as a primary source of Buddhist teaching. A readily accessible English translation is John Ross Carter and Mahinda Palihawadana, trans., *The Dhammapada* (New York: Oxford University Press, 1987). See also Eknath Easwaran, trans., *The Dhammapada* (Tomales, CA: Nilgiri Press, 2007). English translations of the Dhammapada divide the work into twenty-six named chapters and 423 verses, numbered sequentially throughout the whole work. The Dhammapada is presented in the Pali language as the sayings of the Buddha. Siddhārtha Gautama, the Buddha, is not known to have written anything. The sayings collected here are as remembered by followers over a long period of time before they were written down in this form. While regarded principally as a Theravada Buddhist collection, the Dhammapada is respected and used by other denominations of Buddhism as well.

The epigraph that opens the chapter and a later quotation are from Paul F. Knitter, *Without Buddha I Could Not Be a Christian* (Oxford: Oneworld, 2009), xii, xiii, 215.

Quotations from the Dalai Lama are from his book *For the Benefit of All Beings*, trans. Padmakara Translation Group (Boston: Shambhala Classics, 1995).

The stories of Zen Buddhist masters are from Smith, *The World's Religions*, 129.

Quotations from the Lotus Sutra are from Burton Watson, trans., *The Lotus Sutra and Its Opening and Closing Sutras* (Tokyo: Soka Gakkai, 2009). The quotation from SGI leader Daisaku Ikeda is from his foreword to this English-language edition. Another SGI leader, Bill Aiken, has been especially helpful in interpreting the Soka Gakkai movement.

CHAPTER 7: LEARNING FROM CHINESE RELIGION

Hu Xingdon's comment is from an article by Keith B. Richburg, "An Injured Toddler Is Ignored by Passersby, and Chinese Ask Why," *Washington Post,* October 20, 2011.

The first five passages attributed to Lao-tzu in this chapter are from Lin Yutang, trans., *The Wisdom of Laotse* (New York: Random House Modern Library, 1948), sections 7, 25, 78, and 3.

The remaining quotations attributed to Lao-tzu are from John C. H. Wu, trans., *Tao Teh Ching* (Boston: Shambhala Publications, 2003), sections 7, 9, 29, 31, 30, 31, 17, 44, 46, 33, 64, 38, 49, and 63.

Huston Smith's comment on Confucianism is from his *World's Religions,* 183.

Sayings attributed to Confucius are from Leonard A. Lyall, trans., *The Sayings of Confucius* (New York: Longmans, Green & Co., 1909).

CHAPTER 8: LEARNING FROM SMALLER GROUPS WITH SPECIAL MEMORIES

This chapter treats several forms of religion more briefly, but that does not mean they are not just as central in the lives of their adherents as the religions we have considered at greater length.

The epigraph that begins the chapter is from Smith, *The World's Religions,* 2.

Jain religion is helpfully portrayed in *Responses from IFC's 11 Member Faith Traditions to Questions Common to Each* (Washington, DC: InterFaith Conference of Metropolitan Washington, 2008) and at the Jains' authorized Web sites, www.jainworld.com, www.jain study.org, and www.JAINA.org. The IFC document has helpful brief summaries of each of the eleven member traditions. For the Jain emphasis on attitudinal values, its five major vows, and other details, I have also used the Wikipedia section on Jainism.

In the section on Sikhs, I have quoted from Krushwant Singh, trans., *Japji Sahib,* in Malk Raj Anand, *Japji—The Immortall Prayer Chant* (New Delhi: Abhinav Publications, 1987) and the IFC document. The English translation of the Sikh hymn "Kahe, kahe re ban khojan jayee" is by Rajwant Singh.

The section on Zoroastrianism is also informed by the IFC document article by Zoroastrians Brigadier Behram Panthaki and Kersi Shroff. The central Zoroastrian scripture is the Avesta. See also the BBC account of Zoroastrian dualism at http://www.bbc.co.uk/ religion/religions/zoroastrian/beliefs/dualism.shtml, and "Frequently Asked Questions on Zoroastrianism and the Avesta" at www.avesta.org/zfaq.html. Note also Mary Boyce, *Zoroastrians* (London: Routledge & Kegan Paul, 1979), and Firoze M. Kotwal and James W. Boyd, *A Guide to the Zoroastrian Religion* (Chico, CA: Scholars Press, 1982).

The section on Baha'i is informed by the portion of the IFC document written by Sovaida Maani Ewing of the Baha'i faith. According to Ewing, there are more than one hundred volumes of Baha'i scripture. Of these, he lists the Most Holy Book, the Book of Certitude, and the Hidden Words of Baha'u'llah as most noteworthy.

A number of the insights to be gained by Christians from these religions have already been considered in foregoing chapters; nonetheless, nuances of differentiation warrant further study.

CHAPTER 9: LEARNING FROM ATHEISM

A self-described atheist consultant who was kind enough to read a preliminary draft of this chapter agreed *vigorously* with my hunch that most atheists would not want their atheism to be described as a religion. His reason is that the atheist part of their thinking is simply a disbelief in the idea of God held by others; it is not the positive basis of their believing and valuing. I take that criticism seriously. At the same time I continue to regard atheism as a religious phenomenon, partly because of the intensity with which it is often asserted and partly because it is so central a belief about the nature of ultimate reality. But whether or not it should be defined in this way, what we can learn from atheism contributes to our broader understanding of what we can learn from other religions. My atheist consultant certainly concurred in that judgment.

The classic texts of Marxism include such works as the *Communist Manifesto, Capital, The Economic and Philosophical Manuscripts of 1844,* and *The German Ideology.* In some respects the 1844 manuscripts are most useful in presenting Marx's basic humanism. See *Writings of the Young Marx on Philosophy and Society* (Garden City, NY: Anchor Books, 1967 [German original, 1844]), quotation, 289–90. The works of V. I. Lenin are especially important to the twentieth-century development of Bolshevik forms of Marxism. I have written more extensively about Marxism in *The Great Economic Debate* (London: SCM Press; Philadelphia: Westminster Press, 1977), 55–76.

The section on twenty-first-century atheism is especially informed by Richard Dawkins, *The God Delusion* (New York: Houghton Mifflin, 2006), 14, 347, 12 (quoting Carl Sagan), and 253, and by Christopher Hitchens, *God Is Not Great: How Religion Poisons Everything* (New York: Hachette Book Group, 2007), e-book, 12–13, 21, and 24. The Elisabeth Cornwell article "A Very Atheist Christmas" is from the *The Washington Post,* December 21, 2011.

The Einstein quote is from *Out of My Later Years* (New York: Open Road Integrated Media, 1950), 26. His essay "Science and Religion," from which this quotation was taken, was written in 1939 and 1941.

CHAPTER 10: CAN OTHER RELIGIONS LEARN FROM CHRISTIANITY?

The interpretations of Christianity offered in this chapter, and elsewhere in the book, are my own. I am a "cradle Christian," born and raised in a Christian family and nurtured by this faith and tradition through subsequent years. My own experience is that one's understanding of a faith tradition changes through time. Work on the present volume has been a part of that process in my own life.

One of the best, though also voluminous, introductions to twentieth-century Christian biblical scholarship is *The New Interpreter's Bible: A Commentary in Twelve Volumes* (Nashville: Abingdon Press, 1994). Other scholarly biblical studies are readily available, especially from such publishing houses as Westminster John Knox Press, Fortress Press, Abingdon Press, and Oxford University Press. *The HarperCollins Study Bible: New Revised Standard Version* contains careful annotations.